GALAPAGOS

The Untamed Isles

LibriMundi · LIBRERIA · EDICIONES

We dedicate this book to all people whose aim is to live in a better world, where Nature is still in charge.

GALAPAGOS

The Untamed Isles

Pete Oxford & Reneé Bish

Photo Captions

Front Cover: Male marine iguana in breeding colors, Española Island.

Spine: Male great frigatebird with pouch inflated, Tower Island.

Back Cover: Volcanic eruption - Cabo Hammond, Fernandina Island 1995.

Page # 1: A frigatebird mobbing a blue-footed booby, Punta Pitt, San Cristóbal Island.

Page # 2 & 3: Volcanic eruption - Cabo Hammond, Fernandina Island 1995.

Page # 5: Marine iguana, Fernandina Island.

Page # 7: Swallow-tailed gull in flight, South Plaza Island.

Page # 9: Galapagos flycatcher, Santa Cruz Island.

Design: Juan Lorenzo Barragán
& Lorena Zurita / Azuca
Pre-press and printing:
Imprenta Mariscal. Quito, Ecuador.

Galapagos
The Untamed Isles
By Pete Oxford and Reneé Bish
Text and Photography ©
Pete Oxford and Reneé Bish
ISBN: 9978-44-357-6

First Edition 1999 © Natural Highlights Publishing.
Casilla 17-07-9668, Quito, Ecuador.
E-mail: pete@peteoxford.com
Second Edition 2001 © Natural Highlights Publishing and Ediciones Libri Mundi Enrique Grosse-Luemern. Quito, Ecuador.
Third Edition 2005 © Natural Highlights Publishing and Ediciones Libri Mundi Enrique Grosse-Luemern. Quito, Ecuador.
E-mail: librimu3@librimundi.com.ec

The publication of the map of the Galapagos Islands has been authorized for this book by the Instituto Geográfico Militar - Autorización No. IGM - 9907008, del 7 de Julio de 1999, Quito, Ecuador.

Contents

Foreword

We are entering a critical time for the future of the biodiversity of Galapagos. Island archipelagos act as barometers for change in the world. The global human population is increasing, economies are growing, marine and forest resources are being depleted, wilderness areas are decreasing, and pollution is increasing. In the Galapagos, human population is increasing, tourism is increasing rapidly, marine resources are being depleted, pressures are growing on the terrestrial and marine protected areas, and pollution events are becoming sadly more frequent. The Galapagos of the next fifteen years could resemble the Hawaii and Caribbean of the present; including the continuing battles against invasive species, large hotel developments, and the extinction of large percentages of the famous Galapagos endemics. However, if we act now we could possibly avoid this future and ensure the conservation over the long term of the extraordinary biodiversity of these enchanted islands.

The purpose of Pete and Renee's book is to present the views and realities of Galapagos today. Pete's photographs are an artist's representation of the extraordinary wildlife of the Galapagos; they not only capture the wildlife as many have seen it, but each photograph is set with a master's eye. The text describes the situation in the archipelago and is based on over 20 years of experience with the islands. Key within the book is the recognition that the people of the Galapagos represent the future solution for the conservation of the islands. As such the book is a unique view of the archipelago based on photographs of the wildlife that are often seen on a typical cruise but with a text based on a behind the scenes understanding of the islands.

The Galapagos Islands face urgent challenges to a sustainable and conservation oriented future. Latterly, human population growth and economic growth have been exponential and the present development model appears unsustainable. There are substantial and limiting conflicts in fisheries management which contribute to a lack of collaborative local action in the islands. In addition, historical and potential new invasive species continue to be a major threat to the native biodiversity. The solutions to these challenges will require strengthened local institutions to work cooperatively to ensure informed decision making resulting in equitable and sustainable development. Local institutions will only be able to work together when conflicts are reduced and managed effectively and local residents begin to work together for a shared common vision. Part of this vision for the future must include building an island culture that understands natural resource limits; conserves energy, water and essential resources; and critically builds a local constituency for long term sustainability.

I hope that this book will remind you of these extraordinary islands and will also encourage you to take joint action with the institutions of the Galapagos to ensure a sustainable future that balances the needs of people and biodiversity and where the biodiversity of the islands is conserved over the long term.

Dr. Graham Watkins
Director,
Charles Darwin Research Station
Puerto Ayora, Galapagos

Sea lion mother and young, Española Island.

Authors' Preface

In this book we have attempted to consider the Galapagos Islands as a whole, without burdening the reader with loads of facts and figures, or with long, complicated biological life histories of the plants and animals. A book this size could never hope to be a complete treatise of the islands. This is not a wildlife guide, nor did we intend it as such. Other works are already available, many of them excellent, and these we have included in the bibliography.

With this portfolio of photographs, in an unashamed celebration of the Galapagos, we have tried to capture the essence and the spirit of this remarkable group of islands. We have attempted to inspire a sense of awe and simple pleasure as the reader shares with us momentary and commonplace events in the everyday lives of the animals and plants, which we have captured on film. In addition, we have included a record of the volcanic eruption of Fernandina in February 1995, which we have also interpreted as a regular event (albeit on a geological time scale), fundamental to the soul and character of the archipelago.

We have divided the text and photographs into four geographical regions, namely, the western, northern, southern and central isles, in which we have included representative typical sites within the groups.

We have not attempted to offer an 'indepth' underwater coverage of the islands, although a few shots have been included for the benefit of the thousands of visitors every year who experience as much joy underwater with mask and snorkel as with camera and binoculars above.

Our greatest hope is that the reader be able to pick up this book at any time and open it to any page and simply enjoy. We hope that it will release a flood of memories to those who have visited the islands, and create a desire to do so in those who have not. We have also tried to create a sense of understanding of the archipelago without having dwelt too heavily on the serious threats facing the national park. Instead, we have attempted to highlight the beauty and uniqueness of the islands and, in this way, contribute to efforts to conserve their sanctity.

Sally lightfoot crabs and marine iguanas, Santiago Island.

Introduction

The Galapagos Islands are, without question, one of the most important natural history sites in the world. Straddling the equator in the mid-Pacific Ocean 1000 kilometers west of mainland South America, the group is made up of thirteen major islands, each at least fourteen kilometers square. There are also six smaller islands greater than one square kilometer and over forty rocks and islets. Almost entirely volcanic in origin, the islands have risen directly from the ocean floor. In order to understand the composition of the fauna and flora of the archipelago, it is critical to keep in mind that the islands have never been connected to a mainland source of colonization.

Hailed as a living laboratory, the archipelago rose to fame through the writings of British naturalist Charles Darwin. Significantly, today they have been declared a World Heritage Site by UNESCO and have become a mecca for nature-loving visitors.

The age of the archipelago is uncertain. Using potassium-argon dating methods, geologists have been able to determine that the oldest emergent rocks came into being between three and five million years ago. These are to be found on the island of Española in the extreme southeast. The westernmost island of the group (excluding Darwin and Wolf Islands), the island of Fernandina, is much younger, however, and has been dated at only 700,000 years. Indeed, there is a general progression of age towards the east. This age differential between the islands is very well explained by the "hot spot" theory proposed by geologists. The Galapagos archipelago is situated at the confluence of three tectonic plates, the Nazca, Pacific and Cocos. Consequently, as these plates move, the islands which rest on them move as well. The three plates are moving in different directions at different rates. The net movement of the Galapagos Islands is about seven centimeters per year southeast, towards the mainland. However, geologists propose that there is a weakness in the earth's crust more or less where the island of Fernandina lies today. Intermittently, for reasons as yet unknown, boiling magma breaks through this weak point, or hot spot. The result is a volcanic eruption. Lava is spewed from the vent, first underwater. It then builds up into a submarine cone until

Sea lions, Fernandina Island.

finally the tip of the volcano emerges into the air, cools, and solidifies. This newly formed island, sitting on the Nazca plate, then heads southeast, as if it were on a conveyer belt. An empty space forms over the hot spot and, in time, the process is repeated to form another new island, younger and to the west of the previous one. This is, in reality, a simplistic view of events as it seems that the Galapagos hot spot is relatively weak and horseshoe shaped, and its volcanic plume does not always break the surface in the same position.

One problem for evolutionary biologists was to explain how the Galapagos marine iguana, for example, could have evolved from the common green iguana, yet be so different after the relatively short lapse of three to five million years, the age claimed by geologists for the islands on which it lives. It was evolutionary biologists who suggested to geologists that the Galapagos Islands must be older. When geologists began investigating on the sea bed, they discovered that, in a direct line between the archipelago and the mainland, the sea bed is raised in what is called the Carnegie Ridge. Rock samples from the ridge have revealed that some of the rocks were formed in air rather than underwater. This evidence supports the fact that these eroded submarine mountains were once Galapagos Islands themselves. As they traveled eastwards towards the mainland, the islands were eroded to the point where they disappeared below sea level and out of sight. This was the evidence evolutionary biologists needed and, although not conclusive as yet, does suggest that the original Galapagos Islands were formed a very long time ago and are thus much older than the originally proposed three to five million years.

However old the islands actually are, what we do know is that every new island first emerged from the sea as red-hot lava. The Galapagos Islands are indeed one of the most volcanically active sites on earth belonging, as they do, to the 'Pacific Ring of Fire'. There have been many eruptions over the past two decades, including two in 1979 and one in 1982, 1984, 1987, 1998 and 2005. Even today, the young volcanoes in the west continuously blow steam into the air, smell of sulfur and threaten to erupt. And sometimes they make good on that threat, as evidenced by a recent eruption on the Island of Fernandina which we were able to document in 1995.

Once the new lava has cooled to form an island, the result is nothing more than a barren, inhospitable environment, the canvas on which the paint-

Magnificent frigatebird female in flight, South Plaza Island.

ing will take shape. Onto this raw material begins the long, erratic process of colonization. There are two important stages to the appearance of life on remote oceanic islands: arrival of the organism, followed by subsequent establishment. Many organisms may arrive, but whether they are able to establish themselves or not is an entirely different matter. Consider the case of the iguana. The ancestor of both land iguanas and marine iguanas in Galapagos is thought to be the green mainland species, *Iguana iguana*. It must have arrived on a raft of vegetation, which floated from somewhere like the Guayas River in Ecuador. After 1000 kilometers at sea, the dehydrated and hungry iguana arrives to the barren, rocky shore of one of the islands. In order to survive it must eat. Iguanas are vegetarian, therefore it must find plants to feed on. Not

Brown noddy, Baltra Island.

so difficult, one might imagine. But remember that for there to be plants, they, too, must have previously arrived and established themselves. Only very few plants are able to colonize bare lava; these include the lava cactus, *Brachycereus nesioticus*, and *Mollugo* sp., an herb species. The roots of these "pioneer" plants are able to crack the lava and extract nutrients from it. Together with weathering by wind and rain, the lava is very slowly broken down. As parts of the pioneer plants die, their dead leaves and stems are blown into small crevices in the lava. These tiny pockets of organic material provide for the survival of the secondary colonizers. The process advances slowly and, gradually, the breakdown of the secondary colonizers forms more humus and, eventually, the beginnings of a soil for tertiary colonizers and so on, and so on. Therefore, in order for our iguana to find enough to eat, there must already have occurred an important succession of events on the island on which the reptile happened to become marooned. Without any plant life on the island, the iguana would die. The second vital step is that of establishment. In order for the iguana to establish itself as a viable species, this new arrival must then, somewhere, find another

iguana! Not only that, but it must be another iguana of breeding age and of the opposite sex! Unless the iguana which arrives in the first place is a pregnant female, in which case she has a whole new problem: finding a soft substrate in which to bury her eggs. One begins to understand the incredible degree of chance involved in any form of colonization of remote oceanic islands such as the Galapagos.

Certain factors play an important role in determining the diversity of successful colonizers. These include the distance the islands lie from the mainland, i.e., the nearest source of potential candidates for colonization, the direction of the prevailing winds and marine currents, the amount of rainfall, the topography, the diversity of habitats and the age of the islands. The Galapagos Islands have a paucity of species due to the fact that they have proved relatively difficult to colonize. They may also be said to have a disharmonic fauna with respect to the mainland. What this means is that, although perfect niches are available in the Galapagos for certain animals which live on the mainland, these animals are not represented in the islands. Amphibians and terrestrial mammals are prime examples. There are no natu-

Giant tortoise, Charles Darwin Research Station.

rally occurring amphibians, despite plenty of lush habitat in the highlands of some of the islands, and only nine species of native terrestrial mammals have been able to colonize, including seven rat species (some – nobody is sure how many – are now extinct) and two bats. Both amphibians and terrestrial mammals have a low rate of long-distance dispersal. Amphibians, unlike reptiles such as our iguana, have soft, permeable skin which, in a marine environment (i.e.,1000 kilometers of open ocean), means that the animals dehydrate and die due to osmosis. For most terrestrial mammals this salt-water barrier has also proved too much. Even if they found themselves on a floating raft rather than swimming, they would surely die of thirst en-route. Bats, on the other hand, can fly, while rats are small enough to have occasionally survived the journey, probably on large rafts where sufficient liquids could be obtained by eating the foliage of the raft itself. Rats also happen to be versatile and highly adaptable animals.

Examples of disharmony among plants also abound. Several species may continuously arrive but be unable to establish. Orchid seeds, for example, are minute and very likely often arrive wind-borne to the islands. It seems, however, that orchids have a problem, in that most of them need either a highly specific insect pollinator or a symbiotic mychorrhizal fungus, or both, in order to establish. Since neither of these seems to precede the orchid, its seeds are condemned to certain doom. Presently, only eleven species of orchid have managed to establish in the islands, while thousands of species exist on the mainland. Given time, however, surely more will make the grade. It has been calculated by Wiggins and Porter (1971) that less than four hundred chance instances of arrival and subsequent establishment, over the millions of years in the history of the islands, were sufficient to account for the full complement of the present-day native flora of the archipelago. Of the approximately five hundred and fifty native plant species in the islands, roughly two hundred and fifty are endemic.

It seems incongruous to find penguins and iguanas sharing the same few meters of coastline, or albatross sharing an island with giant tortoises. Many of such apparent anomalies can be explained by the complex systems of marine currents which bathe the archipelago. Driven by both the offshore southeast trade winds and the Coriolis force, surface waters off the coast of Chile and Peru are blown north and west. Deflected by the Coriolis force along the equa-

tor, the water heads west towards the Galapagos. The coastal waters of Chile and Peru can not simply all be blown west, however, without being replaced. This water is replaced by Antarctic water, cold, deep and nutrient-rich, that upwells off the coast of Peru and Chile. The trade winds persist and the cold fertile water continues towards the Galapagos, forming the Humboldt and South Equatorial currents. Water cannot be shunted incessantly west, to the shores of Indonesia and the Far East, without being displaced as well. As it is, the water tends to pile up in the west and is often almost a meter or so higher than in the east Pacific. Some of this water returns as the submarine Cromwell current, the first obstacle which the current encounters impeding its flow is the island of Fernandina. As the current collides with the island, cool, rich, water upwells to the surface, flowing around the island into the Bolívar Channel and also around Isabela Island. Likewise, the relatively cool westerly flowing currents, driven by the Humboldt, also upwell locally. The upwellings are determined by the contours of the bottom topography. The flow of water glances upwards predictably off the submarine rises to reach surface waters in key

Sea lion, Española Island.

20

areas of the archipelago. When these nutrient-rich waters move upwards into depths to which solar radiation penetrates (known as the photic zone), then the process of photosynthesis kicks in, forming huge algal blooms and the beginnings of the food chain. These areas of local upwelling support the highest concentrations of marine-based life forms and it is in such areas that penguins and iguanas feed side by side.

Darwin was the first to publicize the fact that on neighboring islands with similar conditions, closely related, yet different, species existed. It was this observation, and the realization that there had been a divergence of species within the archipelago, that steered him on his way to propose the revolutionary theories of natural selection. How has this process of evolution, resulting in unique species on the islands, occurred? There have been basically two processes at work. First, a simple "drift" by an errant colonizer towards a single new species and, second, the process of adaptive radiation, whereby two, or more, species are formed from the original colonizer. Any individual, or small group of colonizers, represents only a fraction of the genetic diversity contained

Sea lion chasing crabs, Santiago Island.

Adult, juvenile and chick flamingos, Floreana Island.

within the original parent population. Within such small, genetically simple populations, there is much more susceptibility to change and the influence of chance. For example, if a gene were to mutate, as happens at random under natural conditions anyway, this gene would represent a relatively much larger percentage of change within the small founder population of individuals than it would within its parent population of millions of individuals. In a parent population of finches, for example, the mutated gene would be so 'diluted' in the gene pool that it would not 'express itself', whereas it may represent the difference between a small beak or a large beak in ten percent or more of a colonizing population. These changes, which are more rapid in small founder populations, due to random change alone, are referred to as 'genetic drift'. This 'genetic drift', if it continues in isolation without the influx of new genetic material from the parent population (i.e. more colonizers of the same species arriving), will eventually lead to colonizers so distinct that they become a new species.

Displaying flamingos, Floreana Island.

Adaptive radiation essentially takes genetic drift one step further. That is, after a founder population has arrived and established itself on an island, an errant individual (or individuals) migrates to a neighboring island. This small sub-population has an even more limited degree of genetic diversity than the original colonizers. Therefore, the same process of 'genetic drift', away from the original colonizing population, begins. Eventually, the two populations become so different from each other that even if some of the secondary colonizers return to the original island they continue as two separate species. This process may happen repeatedly over the millennia such that, as in the case of Darwin's finches, thirteen different species evolved from an original finch ancestor on the islands. Apart from random 'genetic drift', there may also be active processes of selection acting on the populations. For example, a typical ancestral finch stock arriving to a young island will normally encounter a situation of low predation and low inter-specific competition. The finches will also encounter a wide variety of poten-

tial resources at their disposal. In a hypothetical and simplistic situation, where there are different sized plant seeds available, some small, some large, and only very few of intermediate size, then the finches born with small beaks as well as those born with larger beaks will have an advantage over finches with intermediate-sized beaks. Gradually, the genes for small-sized beaks and large-sized beaks become more dominant than those for intermediate-sized beaks and the two populations diverge, eventually becoming so different that they no longer interbreed and two distinct species are formed. This example grossly over-simplifies the situation. In real terms, one must consider a combination of mechanisms for reproductive isolation by which speciation occurs.

The barriers to reproduction which develop may, for example, be geographical, where a small group of individuals colonizing a neighboring island, or indeed, a different part of the same island, do not encounter each other and therefore cannot mix. Behavioral differences may develop such that groups evolve different songs or different sexually attractive displays, so that one group eventually may not recognize and respond to the other. Temporal

Penguin and Pinnacle rock, Bartolomé Island.

separation, where breeding cycles become out of phase, also leads to genetic isolation. Even physical differences may develop and the two stocks may diverge sufficiently to become physically incompatible. Even if cross-breeding does occur, gene counts may be different and any hybrids which form will usually be sterile or less 'fit'.

Through one or more of the processes mentioned, the Galapagos Islands have become home to a fascinating array of plants and animals found nowhere else on the globe. The islands continue to be extremely important to scientists due, primarily, to the simplicity of the ecosystems. The apparent relative youth of the archipelago, combined with barren terrain and difficult access, has not allowed a large diversity of organisms to colonize the islands and so the various niches remain fairly open. The raw processes of evolution can almost be seen to be working, and are certainly well within the bounds of painstaking and careful scientific study.

When first discovered, the uniqueness of the archipelago was not appreciated. On March 10th, 1535, the Bishop of Panama, Fray Tomás de Berlanga, discovered the Galapagos. He and his crew

Iguana swimming (seen from underwater), Bartolomé Island.

Painted locust, Santiago Island.

were blown off course and found themselves in a perilous, life-threatening situation. Although he did comment on the tameness of some of the animals, and was the first to mention the giant tortoises, the bishop was rather preoccupied with his main goal, which was to find water. Indeed, the scarcity of water on these arid islands has proved to be one of the greatest hardships to overcome for all arriving life forms. Some of his horses and several sailors died of thirst.

Once discovered, various ships repeatedly visited the islands. The archipelago soon became known as the "Encantadas" - the "Enchanted Isles". Due to the strong inter-island currents, unpredictable winds and thick banks of fog which tend to suddenly blanket the archipelago, sailors at the mercy of the winds actually believed that the islands moved in order to deliberately confuse them. When the fog lifted, the vessels would find themselves in different positions relative to the islands, due to the action of unseen currents. This was a little too disconcerting for the superstitious men who thus described the archipelago as "enchanted", that is, bewitched. Coupled with the fact that the Galapagos became a pirate stronghold, the islands were feared rather than revered as they are today.

By the late 1500s, pirates were regularly hiding out in the archipelago, and even using some of the beaches to careen their ships. They used the islands as a refuge and a source of meat and fresh water before setting off on raids, pillaging the coastal towns of Ecuador and Peru. It was the pirates and buccaneers who first began the concerted harvest of the endemic tortoises. They discovered that these giant reptiles would remain alive, stored upside down on top of each other in the holds of their ships, for up to a year without food, a welcome source of fresh meat for the crew for whom anything was better than the traditional fare of salted pork and weevil-ridden biscuits. Over the next few hundred years, between one and two hundred thousand tortoises were subsequently removed for food. The pirates were also the first to introduce non-native mammals. Today this legacy of various introduced mammal species is one of the most serious problems facing the well being of the ecosystems within the islands.

Ecuador officially claimed the archipelago in 1832, and a penal colony was quickly established on Floreana. Only three years later, the HMS Beagle from England made its historic visit. The two distinguished personages on board not only put the Galapagos on the map, so to speak, but also revolutionized the whole of modern thinking. Charles Darwin and Captain Robert FitzRoy R.N. spent a mere five weeks in the archipelago, from September 15th to October 20th, 1835. Darwin visited only Santiago, San Cristóbal, Isabela and Floreana, yet, from such a limited stay, he not only drew examples from the islands on which to base his theories of evolution, but also remarked extensively on their geology and formation. FitzRoy, meanwhile, was so accurate in mapping the coastline that his charts were not improved upon for over one hundred years.

Since Darwin's visit, various colonizers and scientists have come to the islands and, over the years, five islands have become permanently colonized. In 1959 the Galapagos was declared a national park, except for those areas already colonized, and the Charles Darwin Foundation was established. In 1964, the Charles Darwin Research Station was launched. In 1968, the first two conservation officials were sent to the islands and thus began the

Pelican, Isabela Island.

Galapagos National Park administration. Already by 1970 major tourism had begun. A 58-passenger ship, the Lina-A, arrived, and several concrete docks were built at various visitor sites around the archipelago.

Human population growth in the islands has continued, virtually unchecked, to the present day. Most of the increase has been in one way or another a direct result of the huge tourism industry which has developed. Thousands of immigrants have arrived from mainland Ecuador, many because they already have family who superceded them to the islands, the effects of population pressure are mounting and even farms in the highlands of Galapagos are being turned in to condos to accomodate the population which now threatens to pass the 30,000 mark.

Those who make up this huge influx of generally unskilled labor, with their attendant families, are looking to reap some reward from the pot of tourist gold. When no work can be found, the immigrants often find themselves in a worse position than that which they held on the mainland. Hope turns to despondency, and the once-inspired immigrants find themselves in a hand-to-mouth situation as they try to feed their families. Others arrive specifically to fish the lucrative sharks, lobsters and sea cucumbers and, often in disregard for the negative effects which their efforts may cause the national park, over-exploitation of the marine stocks becomes the norm.

As the Galapagos is a province of Ecuador, every citizen of the Republic had, until recently, an equal birthright to reap hoped-for rewards from the high paying foreign tourists. In practice, of course, most of the money does not filter down the social ladder, having been creamed off at source, often not even reaching Ecuador. The last several decades have also seen many people born on the islands, people who, now in early adulthood, are defensive of their rights as Galapagueños. This new generation considers it natural to harvest the marine resources. They did not immigrate to the archipelago with a frontier mentality, knowing its international importance as a wildlife refuge, but were simply born there in a quirk of fate. Understandably, some are angry when restrictions are placed on their fishing activities, and it is no surprise in an underdeveloped country that the rules are broken. Perhaps the real blame lies with immigration policies. Indeed, until recently, there has existed not only a distinct lack of interest in curbing population growth on the islands, but also active encouragement of immigration. Increased air services, gasoline stations, satellite communications and banks as well as government sponsored electricity and propane have all been added for the comfort of any would-be colonizer. Galapagos is no longer the hardship post it used to be and, as more and more people come to live there, the human population pressure is being felt by the unique fauna and flora of the archipelago. The time has come to recognize that the human population is permanent and to empower the residents to protect and become proud of their resource. To treat it as finite, use it sustainably and for them to become their own guardians of their future by keeping out the negative and non sustainable impacts. However, in an encouraging move, the National Congress has recently approved a bill – the Special Law for Galapagos – that provides for certain restrictions on further immigration to the islands. Also, a further step in the right direction has been the initiation of an inspection and quarantine program to reduce to an absolute minimum the introduction of aggressive alien species.

For the visitor, the islands remain a truly magical destination. The enchantment lies in the extreme approachability and tameness of the wildlife. There can be few natural experiences more rewarding than quietly sharing a beach with sea lions, especially when one decides to waddle over, flop its body across your outstretched legs, and go to sleep. Mockingbirds scamper down the beach to greet newcomers to their home as finches fly into nearby bushes and investigate the proceedings. The marine iguanas, meanwhile, snort plumes of salt from their nostrils and look on in disdain. One may approach to within a few feet a male great frigatebird with his bright red gular sac, or throat pouch, inflated to the size of a football. Regardless of your presence, he will stretch his wings to their full span of more than two meters, throw his head back, and, quivering with anticipation, let out his shrill, reverberating call to every female flying overhead. Should he be up-to-scratch, passing the female's scrutiny, she will alight next to him and he will lay a huge protective wing across her back to seal the bond. The list of potential interactions to be experienced with the wildlife is endless. One may swim with sea lions in a face to

Swallow-tailed gull, South Plaza Island.

face encounter, snorkel with sharks and manta rays, watch turtles return to the sea after a night of egg-laying, sit with albatross or stay quietly adrift, surrounded by a pod of forty sperm whales, a whale shark or a hundred leaping dolphins cavorting around the vessel in play. Indeed, the islands are nothing short of a wildlife paradise.

The Galapagos National Park Service and the Charles Darwin Research Station are together going to great lengths to restore the natural balance of the archipelago to that existing before the intervention of human beings. In an effort to protect the habitat, most official visitor sites are serviced by narrow trails which the licensed guides accompanying each group ensure are strictly adhered to. Some of the islands, sadly, are riddled with introduced plants and animals. Many are seriously affected. Isabela, for example, has herds of wild cattle, horses, donkeys and goats roaming the volcanoes. Cats, dogs, pigs and rats are also at large and prey at will on the native fauna.

Red-billed tropicbird, South Plaza Island.

The populations of many of the native Galapagos species are extremely small. Such populations are fragile and need protection from the ravages of the introduced predators. The island of Santiago is another seriously affected island. It is thought that there were once up to 100,000 goats and 10,000 pigs on the island! The national park's funds, however, are seldom adequate; thus, until now the costly eradication programs have not always been feasible. In any event, the situation regarding introduced animals is complicated. Pigs, for example, being rather intelligent animals, have become nocturnal and extremely shy. They must be eliminated before the goats because, with no goats, the denuded vegetation will regenerate, rendering it impossible to find and eliminate the pigs. Another example of the complexity of the situation was illustrated on the north of Santa Cruz Island where packs of feral dogs were attacking the limited numbers of land iguanas. The park decided to act. The dogs were locally erad-

icated in an effort to save the iguanas. Subsequently, however, it was noticed that the cat population increased and this, in turn, reduced the local rat population. Perhaps surprisingly, the cattle population was also seen to increase somewhat as a result of eliminating predation pressure from dogs. The net result is that the introduced animals are in their own state of equilibrium. Rats are extremely damaging and almost impossible to eradicate. Unless all of the introduced animals could be eradicated overnight, which is clearly unachievable, it is almost a blessing that there are a few cats to control the rats. On the other hand, one needs a few dogs to control the cats, and so it goes. The situation is probably permanent and indicates the importance of maintaining unaffected islands free from all introduced fauna and flora.

In recent years, the human impact from fishermen has come to rival that from introduced animals. Lobsters, endemic groupers and sharks have been caught in enormous quantities. The lobsters and grouper are for the home market, while huge numbers of large adult sharks have been killed for the sake of a few square centimeters of fin to satisfy the

Bottlenose dolphins bow riding.

Far-Eastern palate. Sea cucumber fishing has also reached calamitous proportions, satisfying the same insatiable markets. Nobody yet understands the biological consequences of the monumental harvests of sea cucumbers from the archipelago but, as with all uncontrolled exploitation, it is bound to create an imbalance somewhere in the food chain. Today sea cucumber exploitation is close to the point of commercial extinction. A major subsidiary problem to the industry has been that fishermen set up illegal camps in sensitive areas such as Fernandina Island. These camps usually involve a high degree of infrastructure. Already Fernandina, perhaps the world's largest (almost) pristine island, has had escaped hunting dogs roaming free over the island, and live goats have been brought on as food. The risk of their subsequent introduction, or of rats and fire ants from these uncontrolled visits, is grave. It certainly does not seem fair that while tourists who pay high fees are controlled to the point that even a step off the path is seen as an invasion of the sanctity of the park, some of the fishermen, despite their conspicuous disregard for the rules and ecology of the islands, have proven hard to control due to political pressures. Since a park guard was shot in the line of duty in March 1997, however, the pressure has apparently increased to control illegal activities. Ecotourism, where conducted in a controlled manner, seems to us the only viable, long-term solution to the continued vitality of the Galapagos Islands. At recent rates of extraction and population growth, the Galapagos National Park has a limited future. What was once the paragon of national parks in the world has sadly been in a steady state of decline. We sincerely hope, however, that the implementation of the Special Law for Galapagos, combined with a general change in attitude from a frontier extractive mentality, to a proud, sustainable, conservationalist attitude among the population will lead to a reversal of this deterioration. Our hopes lie with the Ecuadorians themselves, a people with a growing ecological awareness. Fortunately, today there is hope in the form of the many young Ecuadorians who have already joined the ranks of those fighting for the continued well being of this natural resource. We salute them and wish them well - a true victory must come from within.

Perhaps the recent eruptions on Fernandina and Isabela are a message that the power of nature is a force still to be reckoned with and Nature will one day be able to heal her wounds.

Lava flow - Cabo Hammond, Fernandina Island 1995.

Western Isles

In this chapter, the area of coverage includes principally the islands of Fernandina and Isabela, although some of the satellite rocks and islets are also mentioned. Isabela is the largest of all the Galapagos Islands, accounting for more than half of the total land area.

In excess of 4500 square kilometers, Isabela stretches more than 130 kilometers in length and is over 75 kilometers at its widest point. Whereas most of the other islands in the group represent the emergent tip of a single, largely submarine volcano, Isabela is actually a coalescence of six different volcanoes, each probably formed separately but close together, both temporally and spatially. The result is a wonderfully dramatic skyline, each volcano sitting proudly next to its sibling. The five main volcanoes, namely Cerro Azul, Sierra Negra, Alcedo, Darwin and Wolf stand 1100 meters or more in height. Volcán Ecuador, which straddles the equator along with Volcán Wolf, is largely eroded, half of it having fallen into the sea.

Across the Bolívar Channel to the west, the island of Fernandina is the youngest in the archipelago. Certainly one of the most important islands, it is also perhaps the most impressive. As one stands on the fresh black lava at the edge of the 'aa' lava field ('aa' pronounced 'ah ah', is an Hawaiian word meaning pain, and has come to refer to very jagged and broken lava) at Punta Espinoza on the northeast of the island and looks southwest towards the volcano, one looks out over a dark, barren, dramatic landscape. The volcano rises from the ocean to form what geologists refer to as the 'upturned soup plate' shape of classic basaltic, oceanic shield volcanoes. It sits in a somber mood against the sky, reminding us of the power of the natural forces responsible for its creation. Behind the green facade of mangroves which line the shore, the outlook across the island to the summit of the volcano is indeed hostile. The 'aa' field in the foreground, of sharp and twisted clinker plates, jutting two meters or more into the air, creates an imposing terrain. The more stable areas of lava have, incredibly, become host to one or two isolated plants, principally grasses, the herb *Mollugo* sp. and the endemic lava cactus

Dripping lava - Cabo Hammond,
Fernandina Island 1995.

Brachycereus nesioticus. As mentioned in the introduction, these pioneer plants are incredibly important in the initial stages of soil formation and animal colonization of the islands. Apart from the few such specialized plants, very little other life manages to survive on the 'aa', and not until the gaze falls upon the slopes of the cone itself can a few sparse trees be seen clinging to an existence, relying largely on condensation and mist to satisfy their 'thirst'.

The visitor arriving by boat usually concludes that vegetation is lush on the island after noticing the dense stands of green mangroves lining the shore. These hardy plants, however, derive all their sustenance directly from the sea and use the island only as a point of anchorage. The red mangrove, particularly, is of great importance for its complex system of roots grows seaward forming baffles to dissipate wave action. As the force of the wave is diminished, the more slowly moving water is able to support less particulate matter which therefore sediments out. Mud builds up behind the roots and, subsequently, the mangroves also advance. Land reclamation is only one important service provided by these root systems; they also play host to an infinite number of larval marine species. Fish fry, young shrimp and molluscs all use the still-water areas created by the mangroves as nurseries. In addition, given that the spaces between the roots are too small to allow the entry of large fish, the root system can be likened to a giant sieve which strains out the predators allowing the larvae to grow in relative safety. On Fernandina the mangroves appear to be growing slightly inland in certain areas due to the fact that the ocean has channeled through the lava cracks to form pools of full strength sea water which allow the growth of the salt-tolerant plants. None of the four mangrove species in Galapagos are endemic. Their seeds are highly salt tolerant and, once having fallen into the ocean, will remain afloat for weeks until, through

Erupting parasitic cone, Cabo Hammond, 1995.

Cowley Island.

the action of the wind and currents, they are washed up on another shore, possibly thousands of kilometers away, where they eventually germinate. Due to their very high tendency for long distance dispersal, mangroves are often some of the first colonizers on newly formed foreign shores.

The southwestern coastline of Fernandina also recently extended towards the sea, this time not due to the actions of mangroves but to a dramatic few months of volcanic eruption. In early 1995 hundreds of visitors were lucky enough to witness this incredible, primeval display of Nature's power. As small tourist boats bobbed humbly on the ocean in front of the spectacle, dense pillars of white steam billowed skyward to block out the sun. The long, slow swell from the Pacific lazily crashed over the glowing red river of molten lava, causing hideous explosive reactions. During this eruption, the poor creatures in the area had no idea of the significance of the huge pyroclastic displays around them and would walk across the lava onto a red-hot floe and burst into flames. Truly a

Common dolphins, Bolívar Channel.

spectacular site, it was a parasitic cone on the southwestern flank of the volcano which erupted. For several months, molten lava and volcanic bombs were flung eighty to one hundred meters into the air. The red-hot lava spewed over the edge of the cone and ran in a fast flowing river, more than thirty meters wide in places, towards the sea. Everything in its path was destroyed. Trees exploded into flame on contact, while various animals and birds were also engulfed. On reaching the sea, numerous fingers of the main floe poured into the ocean. As has happened many times before in the history of the islands, the red-hot lava hissed on contact with the water while the sea boiled and turned to clouds of steam. Only a kilometer or so away, a large colony of Galapagos fur seals and the rare Galapagos flightless cormorants, like the iguanas, were oblivious to the enormous forces of both destruction and creation going on all around them. Slowly the island grew.

Fernandina is still incredibly active. It is the youngest island of the archipelago and the closest

Male Galapagos flightless cormorant offering seaweed to female, Fernandina Island.

Galapagos flightless cormorant on nest, Fernandina Island.

Galapagos flightless cormorant and chicks, Fernandina Island.

to the proposed hot spot explained earlier. Due to its youth, it has not yet undergone sufficient colonization to be as diverse as its motherly neighbor, Isabela. Luckily for the island, when Fernandina rose from the sea it did not quite become large enough to close the gap of the Bolívar Channel and fuse with Isabela. It is only this isolation which has prevented the colonization of Fernandina by introduced mammals, the fate of many other islands. To this day, Fernandina still remains relatively pristine - but for how long?

The Galapagos populations of birds and animals are generally very small. Although stable, many species are extremely fragile. Their very existence hangs precariously in the balance so that the slightest intervention by man could tip the scales and quickly render the species extinct - forever. Two vulnerable populations that quickly come to mind are those of the flightless birds in the archipelago. Galapagos is host to the most northerly penguin population in the world.

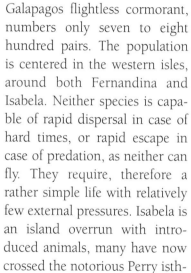
Flightless cormorant drying wings.

The only entirely tropical penguin species, and the only one which actually breeds just into the northern hemisphere, it is naturally enough called the Galapagos penguin; its total population is less than 1,000 breeding pairs.

The other flightless bird in the archipelago is a cormorant. This unique bird, known as the Galapagos flightless cormorant, numbers only seven to eight hundred pairs. The population is centered in the western isles, around both Fernandina and Isabela. Neither species is capable of rapid dispersal in case of hard times, or rapid escape in case of predation, as neither can fly. They require, therefore a rather simple life with relatively few external pressures. Isabela is an island overrun with introduced animals, many have now crossed the notorious Perry isthmus, an extensive 'aa' field lying between Volcán Alcedo and Volcán Sierra Negra, which for some time was hoped to prove an impenetrable barrier to non-native fauna. Rats, cats, goats and donkeys

Sierra Negra volcano's crater, Isabela Island.

are all now beyond the barrier, having followed the coastline and migrated north from the centers of human population in the southeast. The New Scientist Magazine stated (15 April 1995) that the number of feral goats on Alcedo increased from about 10 in 1982 to a staggering 100,000 in 1995. The goats, of course, are a serious threat to the tortoises. They browse the vegetation to beyond the reach of the reptiles and seriously deplete their food supplies. We were even told recently of a guide sighting a goat actually standing on a tortoise, using it as a platform in order to increase its reach - the height of audacity. Project Isabela however is in the process of a huge, concerted effort to eradicate the goat population. The big problem for the birds, however, is the predatory rats and cats. Unable to escape, the Isabela populations of flightless birds are particularly vulnerable. Being unaccustomed to any threat of terrestrial predation, the birds are oblivious to the dangers and take little action in their own defense when at risk. We have watched, on more that one occasion, a cat walk across the backs of marine iguanas to reach a blue-footed booby chick which did nothing to defend itself and was eaten. Fernandina remains the last safe bastion for many species where such threats are nil. The island's importance in this respect cannot be overstated.

Although most of the penguins live around the western isles, some do occur also in the central islands, notably, a small population around Bartolomé island where they are actually more easily seen. Penguins are cold water species, which is why they concentrate in the west where the ocean water is coldest and richest in nutrients. It seems incongruous, nevertheless, to see penguins at home on bare, black lava (side by side with cactus), directly under the equatorial sun. They are *Spheniscid* penguins, related to the Jackass, Humboldt and Magellanic species. Like all *Speniscids*, they are black and white, diminutive in size, bray rather like donkeys, and live and nest in burrows. In the case of the Galapagos penguins, as there is little suitable soil at sea level around their breeding areas in which to burrow, they have taken to using lava crevices for shelter and nesting. Said to be flightless, penguins really do fly underwater. Their wings have adapted to become true flippers and, on close inspection, the tiny feathers with which they are covered are visible. The body feathers of penguins are strongly curved so that they lay neatly on top of one another with

Marine iguana head bobbing, Fernandina Island.

Marine iguana, Fernandina Island.

Marine iguana, Fernandina Island.

a large degree of overlap, like the tiles of a roof. This arrangement helps to trap air, which acts as an insulation layer to keep the penguin warm when it dives. To overcome the added buoyancy of the trapped air, however, penguins often swallow stones to act as counter-weights.

Of the 29 species of cormorant in the world, the Galapagos flightless cormorants are the largest and the only species without the power of flight. Underwater their vestigial wings are held close to their sides, and they paddle with their very muscular legs and webbed feet. They are not pursuit feeders but make a living by foraging in the submarine cracks and crevices between rocks. Their favorite prey is the moray eel and the octopus, which they capture with a swift strike of their powerful head and neck, using the sharply hooked bill to retain the prey. The cormorants are highly local in their distribution, barely ranging more than a kilometer from their natal shores. They have a variable nesting season, but the courtship, if witnessed, is something to remember. In the water, the cormorant uses a rattling call to attract a mate and then the two entwine their necks and rotate energetically on the surface until the pair-bond is formed. The nest is built on the bare rock close to the water's edge and is a scruffy construction comprised mostly of seaweed. At each reunion with his mate at the nest, the male brings an offering of more seaweed which, with great ceremony, is accepted by the female and added to the nest. After laying, both adults incubate the three eggs and raise the young. One of the most characteristic images of the Galapagos Islands is the sight of a cormorant, having returned to land after a spell at sea, with its vestigial wings 'hanging out to dry'. Although useless for flying, the cormorant's wings still serve a slight function as balance organs used when the bird hops from one rock to the next. Cormorants do not produce sufficient oil to water-proof all of their feathers and so do not suffer increased buoyancy from trapped air as do penguins. Therefore, the wing, as it is not water-proofed, must be properly dried out or the feathers will be damaged. Another remarkable characteristic of the flightless cormorant is the piercing gaze of its intensely turquoise eyes.

As unique as they may be, the cormorants are upstaged by perhaps the most quintessentially Galapagos species of them all, the marine iguana. The only truly marine lizard in the world, visitors to the islands are reminded of miniature versions

Great blue heron preying on marine iguana, Fernandina Island.

of the dragons of fairy tales. Of all visitor sites in the archipelago, Punta Espinoza, on Fernandina Island, is the marine iguana capital. On early morning arrival to the site, one finds densely packed marine iguanas 'spread-eagled' over the rocks. Darwin's 'Imps of Darkness', the iguanas lounge over huge areas and blend imperceptibly with the rock itself. As one approaches, a sporadic burst of sneezes issues from the prostrate iguanas. In a 'fight-or-flight' response to a potential threat, the large reptiles clear their nasal passages of a concentrated salt solution enabling them to breathe more deeply if need be. The solution is expelled explosively as two jets of salty spray, one from each nostril. A marine iguana, like a seabird, has a special salt gland in its head which is able to rid the body of excess salt ingested by the animal as part of its daily life. Better adapted than kidneys for the job, the salt gland is equipped with an osmotic pump to extract salt up to twenty parts per thousand more concentrated than seawater.

Marine iguana swimming, Fernandina Island.

The iguanas, particularly the large ones, go out to sea to feed. They dive down many feet underwater and, while clinging to the rocks with their strong, sharp claws, graze the marine algae. Being poikilothermic, or cold-blooded, they must regularly return to shore, however, to recharge their solar battery. The iguanas prefer grazing at low tide so they don't have to immerse their bodies in the frigid waters around the western isles and, in so doing, increase the time of their feeding. They have slightly protruding tricuspid teeth which enable the animals to crop the 'sea lettuce', *Ulva* sp., very close to the rock surface. Iguanas will unhesitatingly swim from one grazing area to the next if necessary, a behavior for which they are admirably evolved. During swimming, the limbs are held passively at the sides of the body while the full propulsion of the animal is derived from the undulating tail which describes a series of sinusoidal curves. The tail itself is dorsoventrally flattened, that is, from back to belly, to present a large surface area to the paddle-like organ.

Male iguanas are larger than females and, during the breeding season in the hot summer months, they aggressively defend a small territorial area of rock favored by females. The males display their might with frequent deep head bobs. Dominance is achieved by vigor, and similarly matched individuals compete in a trial of strength by shoving. The raised scales on the crown of the iguanas' heads interlock as one male tries to push the other out of the disputed area. After the breeding season is over, the females also become antagonistic towards each other. They retire to a sandy area where they dig a tunnel in which they lay two to four leathery eggs. They then aggressively defend the nest site from other females who otherwise might destroy the eggs during an excavation of their own. Once the danger has passed and all the females have laid their eggs, the nests are abandoned and the young are left to their own devices with no further parental care.

The young are constantly in peril after hatching. They hide in lava cracks where they try to remain undetected. Galapagos snakes and herons, particularly the great blue heron, are their main

Galapagos tortoise sleeping on Alcedo volcano.

predators; an experienced great blue heron can eat many hatchling iguanas in a single day. Endemic Galapagos hawks also take young iguanas and will, on occasion, also tackle an adult, particularly the females exhausted after nesting. In general, however, once having reached adulthood, the iguanas are free from predation and actually welcome visitations from birds, such as finches and mockingbirds which, along with Sally lightfoot crabs and lava lizards, prey upon any infestations of ticks and external parasites as well as feeding on molting skin.

The western isles are also home to the second major group of reptiles inhabiting the archipelago, huge animated boulders living on the volcano rims. More Galapagos giant tortoises live on the island of Isabela than on any other in the Galapagos. Each volcano has effectively become an island in its own right. The tortoises do not cross from their native volcano to another, not even to volcanoes on the same island. Due to this relative remoteness and

Galapagos tortoise on Alcedo volcano.

isolation, the tortoise populations on each volcano have gradually drifted apart over the millennia, so that the gene pools have changed and individual groups have become subspecies of one another. Today it is estimated that the total Galapagos giant tortoise population stands at about fifteen thousand individuals divided into eleven subspecies.

The largest population is on the volcano of Alcedo, numbering approximately three thousand individuals reaching up to 225kgs (500 lbs) in weight. Some of the individuals alive today may even have been around when Darwin made his visit to the Galapagos. Many individuals have also died since then. Hundreds of thousands of these dinosaurs were removed over the years by pirates, buccaneers and whalers for whom they were a source of fresh meat. The original population probably stood in the order of two hundred and fifty thousand. As the visitor climbs Alcedo, he or she will begin to encounter the tortoises half way up the slopes

Galapagos hawk, Isabela Island.

towards the rim. Thanks to their dome-shaped carapaces, they can bulldoze their way easily through the dense vegetation in which most of them live. With a relatively slow metabolism, however, they spend a lot of time at rest and, in the warm months, particularly during the heat of the day, under shade. Tortoises love water and mud. When it is available they will spend hours at a time in a wallow which also helps in the removal of ectoparasites. Surprisingly, mosquitoes and ticks can bite even through the shell of the tortoise where they tap into the growing edges of the scutes which have a large blood supply. All along the trail to the rim of Alcedo one can see evidence of tortoises: paths of flattened vegetation, large grassy scat and tortoise-sized sandy pits where the animals have spent the night. Every now and again a tortoise is encountered in the middle of the trail, slowly and deliberately feasting on the lowly plant life. Rhythmic dull thumps and the sounds of 'snoring' can be heard occasionally. Apart from a sudden hiss which the tortoise expels as it quickly retreats into its shell in defense, these sounds are its only vocalizations. The thumping is the bump of the male's concave plastron banging against the rear of the female's carapace as he mounts her. The 'snoring' is actually a grunt, an expression of the effort involved in the act. Matings may last several hours if undisturbed. When the female is ready to lay her eggs, she will wander off on her own looking for a suitable spot. There she will dig a hole with her hind legs, deposit up to sixteen large spherical eggs the size of tennis balls, and then urinate over the covered nest to create a muddy layer which hardens to a solid, protective cap. Like most reptiles, she subsequently abandons the eggs and young who must fend for themselves. Though they seem passive, tortoises will sometimes become quite aggressive towards one another. Males, in particular, compete over females and food resources. A typical display of aggression is a head-on approach with necks outstretched. Once face-to-face, the contenders raise themselves up as high as possible in a threatening posture with mouths agape. He who is tallest is the winner and the shorter animal backs down.

Once reopened the effort of the climb up Alcedo to see the tortoises is definitely worthwhile. There is something very special about sitting a few feet from such a creature, a window on the past, especially in its natural environment, that of a huge volcanic crater. Of course, tortoises

Green turtle, Fernandina Island.

are not the only animals one might see. While walking up the path, the visitor will be accompanied by mockingbirds and hundreds and hundreds of endemic Galapagos finches of many different species. In fact, Isabela boasts ten of the thirteen Darwin's finches, while Fernandina is home to nine. The two islands are also the only home of the rare mangrove finch which today is possibly under threat from over-exploitation of mangrove wood used illegally for fuel by fishermen. This dead wood is the habitat of the wood boring insects the mangrove finch feeds on. Though diminutive and dull in appearance, the finches are very curious little birds, often gathering in large flocks to watch unusual comings and goings.

Lava heron hunting.

The habitats on the hike are varied. The path winds through areas of *Opuntia* cactus and *Scalesia* sp., then lush forests of *Bursera* sp. and *Pisonia* sp. festooned with lichens like old men's beards. The endemic Galapagos flycatcher is another attractive bird to look out for, while its cousin, the vermillion flycatcher, cannot be missed. The male vermillion flycatcher will often be seen calling from the high point of a tree or energetically trying to attract a mate with its acrobatic display flight. The brilliant red of the male is indeed striking, while the female is dressed in a pale lemon yellow. Galapagos hawks are in evidence throughout the walk, often flying down for a closer inspection of passers by. They have even been known to land on tourists' heads, so tame are they! Spiders, grasshoppers and endemic carpenter bees are also common. The black female bees vastly outnumbering the rarely seen orange-colored males.

On returning to the arid areas of the coast, the visitor sees snake-like trails crossing the path. These tracks are made by the tails of rambling iguanas. Land iguanas live mostly in this region, foraging on the succulent vegetation of the area. Of the two species of land iguana in the Galapagos Islands, the most wide-

Land iguana, Isabela Island.

spread is *Conolophus subcristatus* which is also both the largest and most brightly colored. Like their marine iguana relatives, the land iguanas are also vegetarian. They are stockier animals, however, and their color ranges from yellow to brick red. The nose is longer and more typical of the *Iguanidae* family than is that of the marine iguana, while the tail, which does not function as a paddle, is simply round in cross-section. The crest is shorter than its cousin's, and not nearly so ominous. Although there are many land iguanas on both Isabela and Fernandina Islands, Plaza and Santa Fe in the central isles are both much easier sites in which to see them.

The coastlines of the islands are where most of the biological activity occurs, and Fernandina is a favorite area for combing the shore. A magnificent frigatebird will occasionally sit on a dead mangrove, on the lookout for any opportunity to feed. Lava herons stalk the strand, freezing to a motionless statue at the first sign of

Sea lion mother and pup, Fernandina Island.

small fish (staring into a tide pool in absolute concentration, its neck held sprung at full recoil, ready for a lightening strike at its prey). Green turtles inhabit the same waters. Trapped in tidal lagoons as the ocean recedes, they lie a few feet below the surface under rock ledges. When forced to breathe, they gently rise, push their head through the skin of viscous water into the air, extend their neck backwards and inhale deeply. With complete grace and a sense of deliberation, they once again return to their submarine slumber. Sea lions have nursery areas under the mangroves, and the young pups are left to cavort and play under the direction of just one or two mothers during a receding tide, while the others go out to sea to feed. The tide pools offer the pups a perfect playground in which to learn the skills of coordination needed for hunting on their own. Completely isolated from the sea before the tide returns, they are safe in the knowledge that no large marine predators, such as sharks, can attack.

Sea lion mother and newborn pup with afterbirth, Fernandina Island.

Sea lion pups playing in tide pool, Fernandina Island.

The adult females return one by one and it is very rewarding to watch the reunion of the mother with her pup. First she calls and immediately a single pup from the playground sits bolt upright and starts bleating back in her direction. The two come closer, scrambling over the rocks just like a scene from Gone with the Wind, until they finally make contact. Final recognition is established by an elaborate process of nuzzling and whisker touching to confirm one another's smell. When satisfied that the pup is indeed her own, the mother finds herself a comfortable spot on the lava, rolls over and lets her offspring suckle.

The western isles also happen to be home to breeding groups of sperm whales. World renowned whaling grounds in years gone by, the waters off Fernandina have now been declared a protected habitat and the whales revel in the security of their sanctuary. The waters are also known for whale sharks, dolphins and sun fish, while hammerhead sharks concentrate in large numbers around 'Roca Redonda', a lonely outpost to the north. There is something eerie about Roca Redonda (Round Rock): rising out of the deep,

Juvenile pelican, Isabela Island.

dark gray waters, and often clothed in mist, the massive rock looks like a castle, a towering monolith, a monument to itself. Many times, while snorkeling in the area, we have had the privilege of sharing the water with bottlenose dolphins who approach for an appraisal and disappear. Close to the rock, we have also swum with huge hammerhead sharks gliding silently past on outstretched hydrofoils. Despite these wonderful encounters, the waters around the rock somehow hold a sense of foreboding. Perhaps it is their sheer depth. At over two thousand meters, one knows one is in deep water. Perhaps it is also the knowledge that large pelagic tiger sharks are known to inhabit the area. Nevertheless – or perhaps therefore – for us it is Fernandina which holds the most mystery and best embraces the essence of Galapagos.

Adult pelican, Isabela Island.

Tower Island seen from Prince Phillip's Steps.

Northern Isles

In the northern isles of the Galapagos, we have included the remote islands of Darwin, Wolf, Pinta, Marchena and Tower (or Genovesa). The only one, however, with a terrestrial visitor site is Tower, and this is our justification for considering it alone in this chapter. This is truly a spectacular location, and one which, along with Fernandina and Española, should not be missed. Tower is best described, simply, as 'bird island'. Unfortunately most tours to the Galapagos do not include all three of the above islands on a standard visit because each lies at the furthest extremity of the archipelago and the distances involved are great. A typical day on a cruise consists of two visits, either to different islands or to distinct areas of the same island. Once having arrived to Tower, however, changing anchorage and going on to another island for a second visit the same day is out of the question. Luckily, there are two excellent visitor sites available from the same anchorage.

The approach to Tower Island from the south is usually under the cloak of darkness. This is a beautiful pre-dawn experience if the seas are calm and the visitor able to wander around on deck and soak in the ocean's special ambience. Swallow-tailed gulls, the only nocturnal gulls in the world, flit in and out of range of the vessel's navigation lights. Appearing as ghostly apparitions for a few seconds, they quickly disappear. As the boat approaches the island, more and more gulls become apparent, with the curious hovering long enough alongside to display their scarlet eye-ring. The gulls' general progression is shoreward, for they have done their night's work and are returning home to rest and digest their catch of squid. They hurry to return home before daylight, so avoiding the threat of the piratical frigatebirds which swarm in clouds overhead as day breaks.

A cloudless night reveals a plethora of stars from the top deck. Away from artificial lights, the city dweller will be astounded by the sheer number and brightness of the stars in the firmament. Even from above the equator at Tower's position in the northern hemisphere, it is a delight to

Bottlenose dolphin.

spend a few hours and trace the arc described by the Southern Cross as the constellation rises and sets. On a morning with little or no moon, a look over the bow is a revelation: the bow-wave is inevitably alive with bright spots of a cold blue-green light, not the reflection of the stars but light from below, a light produced by planktonic organisms. Many such organisms are able to produce this so called bioluminescence or phosphorescence. Biochemically, the process occurs when, due to a physical disturbance, an enzyme called luciferase is released by the organism. This is a catalyst which acts on a compound produced by the plankton, called luciferin, producing light. It is a process similar to that used by fireflies and glowworms of the terrestrial environment. As the vessel progresses through the water, it causes a huge disturbance to these small planktonic organisms, and they 'fire' their lights in response. The effect is breathtaking. Schools of fish are also 'threatened' by the boat and suddenly scatter in all directions to escape. They too cause the plankton to light up and the result is like a private fireworks display of light guiding the bow. Most impressively, as one arrives close to the island (still before daylight), a pod of dolphins – residents, apparently – often joins the ship. They suddenly appear from several directions, like huge illuminated torpedoes aiming for the bow. Instantly they take up position below the observer, who by now is hanging over the bow in earnest for a closer look at the magnificent phantom performers. Side by side, the dolphins maintain a dynamic formation, keeping just ahead of the turbulent prow, their outlines continuously illuminated by the ghostly light of the plankton. With effortless grace, the dolphins switch positions, roll over and occasionally leap out of the water to almost eye level with the observer, landing with a splash in a seemingly deliberate attempt to soak their private audience and thus include them in the fun. At the first light of day, an orange blush shimmers over the water, and the cold glow of bioluminescence from the plankton dims as the warmth and light of the sun out-compete them in brilliance. By now scanes of red-footed boobies are dipping low over the ocean on their way far out to sea to their favored fishing

Bottlenose dolphins, Tower Island.

Juvenile red-footed booby, Tower Island.

grounds. The shapes of the dolphins can now be clearly made out and even the rake marks from the teeth of fellow dolphins stand out against the uniform gray of the upper body. These are bottlenose dolphins, large – up to three and a half meters in length and 650 kilograms in weight – highly social and intelligent. They come from miles away to play at the bows of passing ships and boats, the dolphins' equivalent of surfing. The movement of the vessel ploughing through the sea pushes water ahead of it. It is in this pres-sure wave that the dolphins ride. They are not actually being pushed by the vessel as many onlookers have imagined. The officer on watch slows the engines as the vessel approaches the island. The cetaceans instantly respond and miraculously disappear.

The island looms ahead. A narrow break in the volcano wall allows cautious access by sea into the once active crater, known as Darwin Bay. The range markers on the far shore are lined up and the vessel steams above the eroded barrier into the

Great frigatebird male, Tower Island.

calm enclosed waters of the bay. Audubon shearwaters zig zag across the wake while storm petrels gently patter on the surface. More and more of the adult red-footed boobies are leaving their roosts in the mangroves and heading out in search of flying fish on the open ocean. The frigatebirds take to the air, but leave the boobies unmolested knowing not to waste their energy attacking an unproductive target. As the boat comes to anchor close to the north wall of the bay, juvenile red-footed boobies land clumsily on the rails and rigging, staring inquisitively with an apparently dumbfounded and shortsighted gaze at almost anything, whether of interest or not. With prehensile feet they are the only Galapagos boobies which are able to properly perch and it is not long before many individuals have graced the boat with their presence. Despite their slightly ungainly and silly appearance when at rest, boobies are magnificent flyers. Even though they far outnumber the other two Galapagos boobies, the red-foots are the least often seen by visitors. But Tower Island is the largest red-

footed booby colony in the world, boasting one hundred and forty thousand pairs. Rather than coming into the center of the archipelago to feed, red-footed boobies fly a long way offshore, which explains why they only breed on the out-lying islands in the first place. They are the world's smallest booby and, because of the distances they fly to catch fish, can only bring back enough food to raise a single chick from each brood, indeed they lay only one egg. Red-footed boobies catch a lot of squid near the surface of the water but seem to have specialized in flying fish as prey. Many times – not only in Galapagos but in all the tropical oceans we have witnessed red-footed boobies swoop down with the swiftness of an arrow in front of the bow of a ship and pluck a flying-fish from midair. The boobies often hang in the air level with the ship on the updraught caused by its forward motion. The instant the vessel disturbs a school of flying fish at the surface, the fish take to the air, accelerating low over the water, like exocet missiles, in a truly remarkable escape response. With its tailfin's lower lobe, the fish paddles violently to create forward thrust while the grossly

White morph red-footed booby, Tower Island.

70

enlarged pectoral (and sometimes pelvic) fins are extended to maintain the fish airborne. The sharp-eyed booby, however, swoops down on the unfortunate victim and, to its complete surprise, snatches it from the air. Adult red-footed boobies exhibit two color morphs, going through life either as a dull brown-bodied bird or a white one. In the Galapagos Islands, only a small percentage of the birds are white, whereas elsewhere in the world the ratio is reversed. Nevertheless both color types of adults have brilliantly red feet together with an exquisitely decorated face. Both the blue skin surrounding the eyes and the pink tinge at the base of the pastel blue bill look as if the bird had applied make-up before leaving the house. The bill's attractive black border adds a finishing touch. The juveniles are less attractive, an ashy brown with dark legs and bill for their first two to three years.

No matter what the age or color of the boobies, they continue to be the universal targets for the scores of marauding frigatebirds patrolling the skies. On their homeward journey before dusk, the returning boobies maintain contact by calling. Incredible as it may seem, the pugnacious frigate-

Red-footed booby perching, Tower Island.

Nesting red-footed booby, Tower Island.

bird can detect the difference in the call made by a booby with a full gullet and one without, as the fish pressing on the throat of the former distorts the sound of its call. They home in on the defenseless boobies, besieging them in dramatic, swashbuckling aerial combat. While the challenged birds fly the gauntlet in a dash for home, the attacks are relentless. Those frigatebirds which have not joined in the chase hang effortlessly on the wing casting an ominous shadow on the scene below. Their silhouettes are reminiscent of competition bows, with arrows at full cock ready to fly. With a span of more than two meters and only weighing in at a kilo or so, frigates have the largest wingspan-to-body-weight ratio of any seabird - the secret to their supreme maneuverability. And with its powerful, strongly hooked bill to complete the arsenal, the frigatebird is arguably the ultimate flying machine. When swooping on a booby, the frigate invariably goes for the tail. With a firm grip it simply shakes the

Galapagos dove, Tower Island.

unhappy victim like a rag-doll in the air. Rather than risk injury from its attacker, the anxious booby has no option but to disgorge its hard-won prize. The frigate releases its grip and swoops to catch the falling fish before it hits the water. Impressive though they are at flying, the frigatebirds cannot either land on, or immerse themselves in, the water as their feathers quickly waterlog and they would drown. The unfortunate booby, meanwhile, returns to its partner empty-handed after a hard day's fishing.

Due to the extremely complicated techniques of food gathering, young frigatebirds are dependent for a long time on their parents, up to one year or more. The young spend a lot of their time sitting forlornly on the small pad of guano encrusted twigs, which was once the nest, waiting for the adults to return. Spread far and wide on the tops of the salt bushes sit other youngsters amid adults in full courtship regalia. There are two species of frigatebird in the

Male great frigatebird with fully inflated pouch, Tower Island.

Male and female great frigatebird together on nest site, Tower Island.

Eagle ray, Tower Island.

Galapagos Islands. The adult male great frigatebird is all black except for the long metallic green scapular feathers flowing off its back, while the female has a white throat and breast and sports a red eye ring. The magnificent frigatebird male, on the other hand, wears purple scapular feathers while the female is distinguished by a black throat and blue eye ring. The *pièce de résistance* of the male of both species, however, is his ability to inflate his brilliant scarlet, grossly oversized gular pouch. The effect is dazzling. During the first half of the year, scores of expectant males display throughout the area of Darwin Bay. In response to an inquisitive female flying low overhead, the unattached males unanimously throw back their heads to maximize the visibility of the pouch; then, with wings at full stretch and shaking with excitement, they pierce the air with their rattling call. The female alights alongside her successful suitor whereupon he jealously embraces her as proof of his prowess.

Great frigatebird chick, Tower Island.

The subsequent nest building is a labor intensive endeavor. The nest itself is a scruffy assemblage of twigs perched a few meters off the ground on a low bush. Red-footed boobies have mastered the ability to break off fresh twigs for their own nests whereas frigates have not. Yet, despite the apparent over-abundance of suitable twigs scattered throughout, they, too, are seriously contested by the frigatebird. Once again, the boobies must suffer the harassment of aerial dog fighting for possession of their hard earned resource. So piratical are the frigatebirds that they will without hesitation steal nesting material even from the nests of other frigates. Indeed, one of the major causes of frigatebird mortality is nests so badly raided that the eggs fall through the gaps and smash soon after they've been laid.

Of the many other avian species which nest on the island, the most attractive are the aforementioned swallow-tailed gulls. These stunning birds

Swallow-tailed gull, Tower Island.

have been described by many as the most beautiful gull in the world. Their instantly distinctive feature is the bright red fleshy ring encircling the large dark eye. Nobody fully understands its function, but the ring probably plays a role in the nocturnal feeding habits of the gull, aiding the bird in detection of the soft bioluminescent light produced by squid and other prey. Many of the world's gulls have a red tip to the bill, a stimulus for the chicks who peck at the red spot, an action that serves as a counter stimulus for the adult birds to regurgitate food. Red, however, is one of the first colors lost at night, so the swallow-tailed gull, a nocturnal bird, not only has a highly visible white tip but also a white base to the bill which serves the same purpose. The nest is a simple accumulation of small stones and coral laid on

Lava gull calling, Tower Island.

the beach or lava. Once hatched, the single chick, which is extremely cryptic in coloration, spends its time under the bushes, or in cracks in the lava, away from the murderous beak of the frigatebird.

One of the greatest revelations of the biology of the swallow-tailed gull is the fact that it may use a primitive form of echo-location to help accurately relocate a landing spot, thereby avoiding a crash landing into the rock face in darkness.

Also living on Tower Island is a relative of the swallow-tailed gull, the endemic lava gull, the rarest gull in the world. The bird is oblivious of its unenviable status and appears locally common. It is not unusual for one gull or a pair of them to spend the greater part of the day either resting on the bow of a moored vessel or quietly sitting on the outboard engine of a *panga*. Their patient demeanor underlies their scavenging behavior as a result of which lava gulls are also doing fairly well around the growing human populations in the islands. Akin to the laughing gull of mainland America, this species' most memorable and unmistakable trait is to suddenly break into raucous 'laughter', revealing the bright orange pigment on the inside of its throat. Normally a territo-

rial display, a pair of gulls often lock into a duet for several minutes, leaving the onlooker in no doubt as to ownership of that particular patch.

Nocturnal yellow-crowned night herons stand stoically on lava ledges around the landing site pretending to be asleep as we, in turn, politely pretend not to see them. When their eyes are open they seem to be in a state of perpetual surprise, perhaps bewildered at seeing strange creatures wandering around in broad daylight.

Tower Island's paucity of faunal and floral species is due to its remoteness: for many species, the island is too distant to be successfully colonized. The shrubby prickly pear cactus, *Opuntia helleri*, unlike the *Opuntias* on the other islands, has soft, hair-like spines which serve no protective role at all. Peter Grant has reasoned that, due to the absence of the Galapagos carpenter bee on

Juvenile yellow-crowned night heron sunbathing.

the island (the cactus flower's usual pollinator), the plant has had to lower its defenses to allow access to birds, particularly Galapagos doves, which pollinate the flowers when feeding on them. Nor have the finches been very successful colonizers of Tower: only four species have succeeded there, namely, the large ground finch, which can often be observed cracking seeds; the large cactus finch, usually with its head probing a cactus flower; the diminutive and almost ubiquitous warbler finch; and the unusual sharp-billed, or vampire, finch. The so called vampire finch has developed a noteworthy trait on Darwin and Wolf Islands where, to sustain its need for liquid, it has taken to pecking wounds at the elbow or cloaca of nesting boobies and drinking the blood! Apparently unperturbed by this blatant act of parasitism, the boobies suffer the assault without complaint. The sharp-billed ground finches on Tower have not yet learnt the tricks of their northern counterparts; indeed, they may never do so. Thus far, they haven't experienced the shortages of fresh water that are prevalent on the more northerly islands.

Another major bird absent from the avian species list is the Galapagos hawk. At the top of the natural food chain in the islands, the hawk is missing not only on Tower Island but on Darwin and Wolf as well. The short-eared owl, on the other hand, has triumphed and managed to settle on all but Wolf. With the absence on Tower of competition from the more dominant Galapagos hawk (perhaps the rarest non-threatened raptor in the world), the short-eared owl has become diurnal. It seems strange to be walking along the eastern plateau above Prince Phillip's steps and come face-to-face with a beautiful yellow-eyed owl in the middle of the day. The resident owls have become expert at preying on the huge numbers of storm petrels sharing the island. Hundreds of thousands of both Galapagos storm petrels and band-rumped storm petrels nest and breed in the area. During the day, mostly Galapagos storm petrels are visible at the colony. They can often be seen in enormous flocks, like clouds of mosquitoes, flitting above their nest sites in the lava cracks. The owls are extremely adept at catching these little storm petrels and have developed a most 'un-owl-like' technique; instead of pursuing them in flight low over the lava, as one might expect, they wait patiently at the entrance to one of the nest burrows wedged between the plates of lava. When a bird emerges

Lava cactus, Tower Island.

Opuntia cactus, Tower Island

Masked boobies' mutual preening, Tower Island.

Masked booby, Tower Island.

Masked booby, Tower Island.

to within range, the owl plunges its whole leg into the crevice and seizes the bird in its talons. Luckily for the storm petrels, the small number of owls on the island does not seem to be anywhere close to making a dent in their enormous population. These diminutive birds (tube-nosed creatures related to albatross) fly above their nest sites in a seemingly chaotic and erratic fashion. Amazing though it seems, with thousands of nest sites in the lava crags, they recognize their own nest by smell!

Tower and Darwin are also unusual due to being the only major islands without any terrestrial reptiles. No lizards, snakes, geckos, tortoises or land iguanas live there. Once again, it seems that the relative remoteness of the islands have proved too much for any successful establishments.

The visitor to Tower will, however, encounter many marine iguanas on the shoreline, though they are often overlooked initially because of their small size. It seems that the relatively tropical conditions of Tower are less than conducive to the growth of their preferred algal food species, resulting in an average iguana body size which is the smallest for any population in the archipelago. The warmer waters from the Panama Basin which affect the northern isles do, on the other hand, lend themselves to more tropical species of fish than are able to survive in the colder upwelling waters bathing the remaining islands of the archipelago. Large schools of king angelfish can be seen during a snorkel along the crater walls, while enormous bumphead parrot fish rise into view from the murky green waters. Gold-rimmed surgeon fish and convict tangs verify the northerly distribution of the island and flash past regardless. Schools of eagle rays are also commonly seen close to shore and, with care, a snorkeler can join the school, working his or her way to the middle and watch the rays swimming all around.

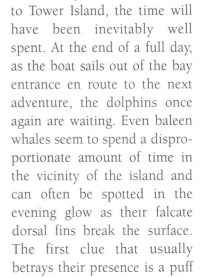

Short-eared owl with storm petrel prey.

Nor should one be alarmed if large moray eels, hammerhead sharks or manta rays are encountered while swimming. All are common in the bay but none has so far proved to be dangerous. The northern isles of Darwin and Wolf have become internationally recognised in recent years as a mecca for scuba divers interested in intimate encounters with large schools of hammerhead sharks which congregate in dense groups of up to two hundred individuals. Whatever the individual experiences of visitors to Tower Island, the time will have been inevitably well spent. At the end of a full day, as the boat sails out of the bay entrance en route to the next adventure, the dolphins once again are waiting. Even baleen whales seem to spend a disproportionate amount of time in the vicinity of the island and can often be spotted in the evening glow as their falcate dorsal fins break the surface. The first clue that usually betrays their presence is a puff of vapor forcibly expelled with each breath. The sun sets on the marine mammals as the vessel leaves them in its wake, on course for somewhere new in the Southern Hemisphere.

Large cactus finch on Opuntia cactus, Tower Island.

Swallow-tailed gull chick with parent.

Cliffs and waves on Española Island.

The Southern Isles

In this chapter the three main islands to be considered are San Cristóbal, Floreana and Española, as well as many satellite rocks and islets of each. In contrast to the young, dramatic islands of the west, with high volcanic peaks and smoldering fumaroles, these southern isles are old, cold, eroded and dormant. The southeastern group, being the oldest present day islands, probably represents the first stepping stones of some of the life forms arriving to the Galapagos from their distant shores of origin. Española is now so eroded that there no longer remains any evidence at all of a volcanic cone.

Two of the three islands are now inhabited by human beings. During the period of human association, particularly in the last two centuries, non-native mammals such as pigs and goats were deliberately introduced to provide future food stocks. Other species, such as rats, were accidental introductions, simply jumping ship and swimming ashore or escaping while the vessels were being caulked and repaired on the beaches. During this period, scientists also took an interest in the archipelago. A scientific mission of exploration sent out from Spain in 1790 was followed shortly by a mission of exploration under the command of English whaling captain James Colnett aboard the vessel HMS Ratter in 1793. Colnett had a commercial interest in the stocks of whales in the area. During this era in Europe and North America, whale oil had become a very valuable product used to fuel street lamps in the cities. Subsidiary products were also coveted, including spermaceti from sperm whales used as a fine lubricant, while the baleen plates of the rorqual whales were used in the manufacture of chique body corsets for ladies of the period. Colnett discovered healthy whale stocks and, at about the same time, the commercial harvest of fur seals for their pelts began. Over the next century, the hunting pressures were so great that not only the fur seals but also some of the whale species were brought to commercial extinction.

Captain Colnett has also been credited with the establishment of the Post Office Barrel on the island of Floreana. It served as a receptacle for mail for crews of whaling and fur-sealing vessels. The

mail was collected by homeward bound ships and, on arrival, was delivered to anxious recipients, predictably more than a year after its deposit in the barrel. To this day the tradition continues as tourists regularly leave mail in the Post Office Barrel which is collected and delivered by subsequent visitors to the bay. Often quicker than the national postal system, the tradition now continues more for fun than out of necessity.

In the 1830s there was an attempt to colonize on Floreana. The settlement quickly turned into a penal colony, an institution more in tune with the harsh environmental conditions prevailing. In 1858 Manuel J Cobos and an associate, José Monroy, set up a company on San Cristóbal to harvest the epiphytic *orchilla* moss used in the dye industry. After this effort failed, Cobos went into the sugar business, planting many hectares of sugar cane and building a sugar mill. As he owned the only boat going to and from the mainland, and the only shop on the island, he had a complete monopoly on the comings and goings of his workers. They were paid not in cash but in tokens, which could be traded only in the shop for goods

Flamingo, Punta Cormorant, Floreana Island.

at inflated prices. Due to the absence of an official law enforcement entity, Cobos quickly reverted to a maniacal tyrant responsible for executing and deliberately marooning people on waterless islands. Unsurprisingly, a bloody revolt ended with his murder and the escape of the enslaved work force. Various other colonization attempts were made around the archipelago throughout the last century, resulting in five islands with permanent human inhabitants today.

The Galapagos has attracted an eclectic mix of visitors in its history. The most famous, of course, was Charles Darwin, who visited four of the islands. He first set foot ashore somewhere in Steven's Bay on San Cristóbal, an area whose appearance has changed very little in the interim. Darwin noted the event as follows: "In the morning we landed on Chatham Island [San Cristóbal], which, like the others, rises with a tame and rounded outline, broken here and there by scattered hillocks, the remainder of former craters. Nothing could be less inviting than the first appearance. A broken field of black basaltic lava, thrown into the most rugged waves and crossed by

Adult greater flamingo, Floreana Island.

Mocking bird attacking turtle hatchling, Española Island.

great fissures, is everywhere covered by stunted, sun-burnt brush wood, which shows little signs of life." After his stay in the islands, Darwin continued on his voyage aboard HMS Beagle, taking with him many rocks and biological samples, together with the seeds of new ideas which, once having flowered, were set to change the course of scientific thinking. Contemporary colonization stemmed mostly from Europe, with Ecuadorian residents not arriving in any significant numbers until much later. During the 1930s a strange mixture of Europeans settled on Floreana at Black Beach near Post Office Bay. The group included Heinz Wittmer and his wife Margaret (she died at the age of 95 in 2000) who arrived with their son Harry. Dr Friedrich Ritter and his mistress Dore Strauch, having arrived

Mocking bird with turtle hatchling.

before the Wittmers, had already molded a distinctive way of life for themselves in their own personal Eden. Friedrich and Dore had met in Berlin and managed to convince their respective spouses to cohabit while they eloped to the Galapagos. In preparation for the sojourn, Friedrich and Dore saw fit to have their teeth removed as a precaution against dental emergencies, but prudently packed a single set of stainless steel dentures which they would share when eating something requiring mastication. A third party to arrive and join the bickering assembly was headed by the Baroness von Wagner who disembarked with three lovers. Many unexplained deaths and disappearances occurred over the next few years, when members of the three parties were the sole inhabitants of the island. Sadly the delightful Margaret Wittmer passed away recently but her daughter and granddaughter, still run both the post office and a modest boarding house. There is now also a naval base at Black Beach on Floreana and a small agricultural community which farms in the highlands.

Although not the largest town in the archipelago, Puerto Baquerizo Moreno, on the island of

Exhausted female green turtle ready to lay eggs, Floreana Island.

San Cristóbal, is the site of the capital of the Galapagos province. Having rapidly expanded in the last two decades, aided by the construction of an airport and increased air services, the town now sprawls a long way up the hill towards the crater. San Cristóbal is the only island in the province which can be considered to have a large permanent fresh water supply which comes from the rain-filled lake known as El Junco. As such, living conditions have always been less harsh than on the other inhabited islands. There is also a naval base on the island, much larger than the one on Floreana. The town's folk rely primarily on tourism and fishing to support their way of life and, apart from serving as an administrative center, the island is an excellent base for both day-tripping tourism and a starting point from which to join a live-aboard yacht tour.

As wildlife viewing in the southern isles is superb, both Floreana and Española islands rank high on the list of sites to be seen. Floreana has several places of interest, both above and below the water. For the snorkeler, a sea lion fantasia awaits at the small islet of Champion. It is simply heavenly to swim there, close to the steeply shelving shoreline, while a multitude of young, curious sea lions, with exquisite grace and agility, frolic playfully, interacting with their awkward audience. Approaching closely for an intimate inspection of the face behind the mask, or an inquisitive nibble of the snorkeler's flippers, the sea lions suddenly shoot off, like living torpedoes, out of view into the depths. A few minutes later they return to continue the inspection and once again disappear. One is never certain who is appraising whom as contact is made underwater with a pair of wide, bright, intelligent eyes.

Devil's Crown, lying just off Punta Cormorant, on the northern shore of Floreana, is an old, eroded parasitic cone. It, too, is a favorite visitor's site. One can swim in shallow, protected areas within the cone, surrounded by

Green turtle hatchlings emerging from nest.

brightly colored tropical fish or, outside, in the current with sharks. The beautiful markings of the stylish Moorish idol, a tricolored reef fish of black, white and yellow adorned with a pennant-like streamer from the dorsal fin, compete with the blacks and yellows of sergeant-majors, or the pastel shades of parrot fish and king angelfish which also abound. The serenity of their watery world is only occasionally disturbed by the large form of a sea lion streaming through the field of view, vying for some of the attention. Outside of the crown, the snorkel starts at the eastern mouth of the cone's broken wall. A steady current carries the passive snorkeler over the bottom. The topography is uneven, with dramatic pinnacles of rock rising from a depth of fifteen meters or so. Large shoals of grunts and creolefish hang mid water, huddled together for protection as the current and swell buffet them to and fro. *Bacalao* (an endemic grouper) and large snappers patrol the rock faces, and schools of barracuda cruise through the water column. Six or seven harmless white-tipped reef sharks slide under an overhanging rock close to the bottom when, suddenly, the adrenaline starts

Pelican, Gardner Bay, Española Island.

pumping as the exact shape of the large dark objects flowing over the sea bed is deciphered by the brain - hammerhead sharks! The novice snorkeler's first thoughts are to return to the attendant dinghy. On the other hand, there is nothing better than to swim down to the group of maybe twenty individuals and have a closer look. Sharks, of course, should always be highly respected, especially large ones such as these scalloped hammerheads of up to three meters or more in length. However, with caution and an understanding of the behavioral cues of aggression, they can readily be approached. Free diving with these huge marine predators is indeed a wonderful experience and accentuates the magic and tameness of the Galapagos fauna. We have even had sea lions follow us down and tease the sharks by nipping their dorsal fins, something they would never dare to do at night when the sharks have the advantage. As the drift continues, green turtles are also commonly encountered lazily flapping their large front flippers, maintaining their course to nowhere in particular. Once having satisfied a curiosity for that which lives underwater off Floreana, the visitor is

Galapagos hawk, Española Island.

Sally lightfoot crab, San Cristóbal Island.

Female lava lizard, Española Island.

Young sea lions, Punta Pitt, San Cristóbal Island.

naturally drawn to explore the remarkable area of Punta Cormorant itself.

The landing beach has a subtle greenish hue imparted to it by the high content of volcanic crystal olivine. After forming in the magma chamber under conditions of extremely slow cooling, olivine is released to the surface during the following eruption. It is subsequently broken down to the consistency of coarse sand by wave action, and sorted onto particular beaches around the archipelago. A short walk behind the green beach leads to a large, saline lagoon. On either side of the path grow some fascinating plants. *Lecocarpus pinnatifidus*, or cutleaf daisy, grows as an erect shrub to about two meters in height. It is a member of the composite family, with large yellow, daisy-like flowers which are in bloom for the greater part of the year. It represents one of seven endemic genera of plants on the islands. A second of these is the *Scalesia* genus, examples of which grow amongst the *Lecocarpus*. At Punta Cormorant, the species *Scalesia villosa* is locally common. *Scalesia* is important for, like Darwin's finches, it provides excellent examples of adaptive radiation (there are an impressive fourteen species with an additional sextet of subspecies). Also known as daisy trees, the various species range from small, isolated shrubs to dense stands up to fifteen meters in height. Another composite, the flowers vary in complexity but are always white. As many of the *Scalesias* occur in the arid and transition zones, they have evolved a coating of delicate hairs on the leaves which are able to trap the fine mist which falls in the *garúa* season.

At the end of the short path, the shallow lagoon offers a perfect flamingo habitat. Numbers range from a few individuals to almost two hundred flamingos at a time which stand out in prominent pinks against the muted background of *palo santo* trees on the slopes of the volcanic cone behind. There are, however, only an estimated four hundred or so individuals in the whole archipelago, making the population rather fragile. They move in groups to various brackish lagoons between the islands in response to the levels of food available in each area. Flamingos are filter feeders. Similar in some ways to the great baleen whales, flamingos actually filter out minute inver-

Bull sea lion, Española Island.

tebrate organisms from the shallow waters and fine silts. The piston-like tongue has a rapid pumping action which draws the water in and out of the beak. In so doing, the prey items, such as brine shrimp and larval crustaceans, are trapped by the fine grooves in the bill. The tongue, armed with a row of spines, serves to rake the food into a bolus prior to swallowing. Although highly specialized, the feeding technique is not particularly efficient and flamingos spend a large part of their day with their heads down in the water, swaying from side to side in their attempt to glean enough sustenance to see them through. The unusual down-curved bill is designed to be used in this manner upside down, so that when flamingos are in the feeding position, the active area of the bill is actually horizontal to the water which, of course, is exactly where it wants to be. The beautiful coloration of the flamingos is enhanced by the pigments contained in the food items. Many flamingos in zoos fade to white unless the high levels of carotenoids are maintained in their diet during molting. The flamingos found in the lagoon at Punta Cormorant also breed there and, looking into the distance

Blue-footed booby, Española Island.

with binoculars, one can often spot small volcano-like cones made of mud. These elevated nests, which the flamingos make for themselves under normal circumstances, serve as ideal platforms on which to raise their single chick. As they are low on the ground, however, they are susceptible to heavy flooding (particularly during an El Niño year) and, unfortunately, raids by feral pigs. The birds sometimes wander out onto the beachfront and feed in the shallow surf zone. Visitors delight in watching such handsome creatures meander, unconcerned, about their business among the onlookers. The chicks and young occasionally follow the adults down to the shore, but seem somewhat ungainly alongside their resplendent parents.

On the far beach, through a forest of *palo santo* and *palo verde* trees, the atmosphere is very different. The beach itself is known locally as the "Flour Beach" and is remarkable for the texture of the sand. Most visitors are encouraged to shed their footwear in order to fully appreciate the phenomenon. The instant the bare feet come into contact with the cool, extremely fine coralline sand is almost sensual. It is a sheer pleasure to walk on, an

Blue-footed boobies diving, San Cristóbal Island.

105

experience not to be missed. On the white sandy areas grow more endemic plants, particularly an unusual endemic succulent called *Nolana*. The top of the beach is deeply pitted with excavations made by nesting female green turtles with an occasional carcass of one of them biodegrading slowly on the shore, a testament to the effort involved in egg laying. At the water's edge the ocean laps a long way up the sand as each small wave breaks on the shore. By carefully shuffling out to a position knee-deep in water, visitors will find hundreds of stingrays sharing the sand with them. They are carried up the beach with each action of the swell, where they feed on buried molluscs and other invertebrates. Some of the rays come to such shallow waters that their backs actually break the surface. Potentially dangerous, these fish, with a wing span of less than one meter, are not aggressive and, like the sharks, if approached with caution are no threat whatsoever. Towards evening, frigatebirds congregate over the turtle nests, patrolling the line of depressions in the sand. With their extremely acute vision, they are able to detect the slightest movement of an emerging turtle.

Dancing blue-footed booby, Española Island.

Sometimes the timing of the baby reptiles goes array and all of the hatchlings break out while still daylight, condemning most of them to death.

On the neighboring island of Española to the east, another fantastic wildlife destination, there are also large areas of turtle nesting beaches. It is the southernmost island of the group and, in many ways, the most unusual. One important turtle beach in particular is the spectacular expanse of Gardner Bay. Many tens, probably hundreds, of female green turtles nest on the narrow beach each year. Thousands of their young also die there. Pelicans sit patiently waiting for hatching time. Frigates keep vigil overhead. Galapagos hawks patrol by walking up and down along the line of salt bushes at the top of the beach. Mockingbirds, however, actively dig them up. At least a score of times we have carefully followed the birds and watched them unearth hatchling turtles. The Española mockingbird is endemic to the island and has the longest dagger-like beak of all Galapagos mockingbirds. It is used with brutal efficiency, serving as the perfect lethal weapon. With its bill, the mockingbird digs in the sand after detecting a slight movement below the surface.

It flicks sand in all directions as it energetically digs down as far as four inches below the surface. Suddenly, with a violent tug, the forcep-like beak grips the baby turtle's head and jerks it out of the sand. Taken under the bushes out of reach of the frigatebirds, the struggling baby is repeatedly flipped onto its back as the mockingbird incessantly stabs it in the soft umbilical area. The fellow gang members of the mockingbird clan quickly descend on the turtle

Blue-footed booby coming in to land, Española Island.

Juvenile pelican, San Cristóbal Island.

Blue-footed booby, Española Island.

Waved albatross, Española Island.

and, eventually, after a harrowing struggle, it is killed. The turtle body is too tough for the mockingbirds to break open so they are able to eat only that which they can reach through the umbilical hole. The carcass is left for ants or hawks, and another turtle is uncovered.

Sharing the fabulous beach with birds and turtles lie lazy, relaxed sea lions. Outstretched on the golden sands at the edge of turquoise waters, like the humans beside them, they seem to have found a certain paradise. A subspecies of the Californian sea lion of circus fame, our Galapagos cousin is every bit as endearing. The females and juveniles tend to congregate in clumps along the beach and, being thigmotactic, they enjoy body contact. Lying on their fore flippers with their hind flippers tucked in under their sausage shaped, hydrodynamic bodies, they orientate themselves with several heads coming together in a point, whiskers touching, or head-to-tail in pairs, with both animals lying slightly on their sides maximizing the area of skin-to-skin contact. Sea lions seem to be very efficient hunters, preying largely on fish, but also occasionally tackling octopus and crustaceans. So efficient are they, in fact, that a large part of their day is spent on a beach at rest. With no pressures to find food, they have time to express their curiosity and, as stated earlier, it is not unusual for a patient observer to become the subject of that curiosity. The young sea lions are particularly inquisitive, often approaching an observer to sniff the face or feet and sometimes playfully even taking the toes gently in their mouths. Nor is it unusual, if the object of interest remains calm, for the sea lion to decide that it is not under threat and lay gently alongside or on top of the legs of its human companion for a nap.

Waved albatross incubating egg.

The main visitor site of Española Island, however, is not Gardner Bay but the westernmost tip, Punta Suárez. This area is home to large numbers of birds and animals and gives a good overview of

Bull sea lions fighting, Gardner Bay, Española Island.

Waved albatross, Española Island.

the islands of Galapagos. The first major attraction on landing are the marine iguanas. Even though the visitor may have seen these reptiles on other islands in the archipelago, none are quite like those of Española. They are of average size and similar shape to their contemporaries, but their coloration is quite different. During the breeding season, in the warm months around Christmas time, the iguanas stray dramatically from the dull blacks of their brethren and become gloriously technicolored. The bulk of their body is imbued with a bright red while their forelimbs and a median area of the back and crest become a garish turquoise, the color of oxidized copper (see cover). The overall effect, however, is very pleasing as the iguanas become conspicuous against the dark lava background. Even outside of the breeding season, the Española iguanas retain a lot of the red base color, setting them apart from those of other islands.

For an as yet unexplained reason, the endemic lava lizards of the island are also the

Waved albatross gamming, Española Island.

114

reddest of the archipelago. Unusual among animals, to the human eye at least, the female lava lizards of Galapagos are more attractive than their male counterparts, sporting varying degrees of red around the head and neck. The female lava lizards on Española have not only a large red area on the head and neck, but also spreading over the throat, chest and forelegs. As the lizards scuttle over the rocks defending their territories or searching for food, they are naturally drawn to the nests of their feathered neighbors where the hunting for flies is better than average.

Two species of boobies nest on Española island, both on the ground. The larger of the two, the masked booby, a startlingly white bird trimmed in stylish black, tends to nest in colonies on edges of islands close to the sea. In contrast to the red-footed boobies mentioned in the chapter on the northern isles, masked boobies are referred to as inshore feeders. They fly away from the islands but do not leave the confines of the archipelago when they go hunting. Like all members of their family, the *Sulidae*, masked boobies are spectacular plunge divers. They shoot like arrows, from fifteen meters or more in the air, onto their

Waved albatross gamming, Española Island.

Galapagos hawk feeding on marine iguana, Española Island.

Galapagos snake, Española Island.

fish prey below. Due to the high impacts suffered at the moment of hitting the water, boobies have some specially adapted features to avoid potential damage. Not only do they have a series of small air-sacs in the head and chest area, but their nostrils are shielded to prevent the force of the dive sending two powerful jets of water into the brain. They have heavy, sharply pointed bills to streamline their entry into the water, and forward pointing eyes providing stereoscopic vision and therefore the ability to judge the distance of their prey. One of the largest birds in the Galapagos Islands, the masked boobies have a wingspan in excess of a meter and a half. The most notorious element of the masked booby's behavior concerns the rearing of offspring. The female invariably lays two eggs over the course of several days, though only one chick will be raised. The nest of the booby is merely a shallow scrape in the ground, which is almost always surrounded by a white guano ring. This ring is formed by incubating adults who, as they rotate on the nest following the sun's motion, squirt guano randomly in all directions. The ring delin-

Blue-footed booby, Española Island.

eates the boundary of the nest. The first chick to hatch has an immediate size advantage over the later arrival. If it is healthy and grows normally, it will quickly become much more powerful than its younger sibling. As soon as it is strong enough, it simply pushes the weaker chick out of the nest beyond the guano ring, whereupon it will be disowned by its parents and killed by predators. Should anything happen to the first chick, the insurance policy kicks in and the second chick descends from death row to grow normally, rather than suffer the consequences of the bizarre so-called 'Cain and Abel syndrome'.

The second booby species to breed on Española is the comical blue-footed booby. They appear to be everywhere on the island, so tame that they have built their nests in the middle of trails, forcing visitors to step over them. When looked at head on, boobies appear to have a very quizzical expression, explaining in part, the derivation of their name, which originates from the Spanish word 'bobo' – which translates as "clown". This species is known as a coastal feeder and rarely leaves sight of the shoreline when

Female sea lion, Española Island.

hunting. They, too, are spectacular plunge divers and often hunt in large groups. As aerial predators, they rely on large predatory fish trapping the smaller prey species against the water surface and therefore putting them within reach of the relatively shallow-diving birds. Without the larger predators the bait fish will naturally favor deeper depths, out of reach of the aerial assault by the boobies (a message that over exploitation of one species can drastically affect another, apparently unrelated species in the food chain). Feeding so close to the nest site, blue-footed boobies, on the other hand, are able to make many feeding forays during the day and therefore bring back enough food to raise up to three offspring if conditions are good. Their most striking feature, however, is their webbed blue feet. When asked, "Why have these boobies got blue feet?", scientists simply reply, "Why not!" They are obviously important as sexual stimuli to mates, but why they should be blue nobody knows. Blue-foots are perfect showmen and a delight to watch. When flying in to a prospective mate or established partner, the males throw back their wings and raise their

Blow hole, Española Island.

splayed leathery blue webs in a flag-like salute just before landing. Courtship begins with rather a lot of vocalization between the smaller, whistling male, and his beefier partner who honks. Apart from size and call, she is easily recognized by an apparently larger pupil. Actually, it is not larger than the male's pupil but there is a dark staining of the iris which gives it this effect. The two birds coyly offer presents, a twig, a stone (something symbolic of nest building), and may also touch bills. A few sideways glances, some ritualistic high-stepping, showing off the blue feet, and the bond is strengthened. The culmination of the courtship is expressed in a series of dramatic, simultaneous skypoints, with beak, tail, wingtips, and everything else that is pointed, on both partners stretched skyward as the two birds face each other and vocalize. In the grand finale and climax of the show, he steps onto her back to bring his cloaca into contact with hers, and they mate.

Once having walked through the large blue-footed booberie on the plateau area inland from the shore, the trail takes the visitor through another, uniquely Galapagos, phenomenon.

Blue-footed booby chick, San Cristóbal Island.

Masked booby pair, Española Island.

There exists on Española a colony of some fifteen thousand pairs of Galapagos waved albatross. Considered endemic to the islands, they spend most of their lives at sea, only returning to land to breed. This is an exquisite bird with the apparent texture of porcelain. The chest area of the adult is delicately marked with a fine, wavy pattern, hence the derivation of its name. Weighing in at an impressive three or four kilograms, with a wingspan of over two meters, it ranks as one of the archipelago's largest birds. The path skirts the outer edge of one of the colonies, offering the visitor superb close-up views of the magnificent birds. Albatross begin returning to the island towards the end of March, usually the males first, ready to start breeding. They spend their non-breeding period off the coast of Peru and northern Chile, where we have seen hundreds at any one time. They pair for life in a monogamous relationship lasting perhaps half a century; it is not thought, however, that they travel with their mate while at sea. On returning to Española, each albatross, must once again find its partner amongst all the other individuals on the island. They do so by gamming (dancing). Amazingly, despite the lapse of time between their last meeting and the present one, they remember how the other partner danced. For the male to reunite himself with his spouse, he must wander through the colony and dance for the females until there is recognition. Needless to say, the dance itself is very complex, highly stylized and immaculately choreographed. It involves a series of behaviors such as 'fencing', 'gaping', the 'shy look', 'swaggering' and a bolt upright stance, the true significance of which is only fully understood by the pair involved. Part of the albatross elegance is a pale, straw-colored area on the head which is offset by the rather large, erectile eyebrows, unusual among albatross and perhaps serving to shade the eyes of the world's only truly tropical species from the intense sunlight. Like all albatross species, these lay only a single egg, weighing approximately two hundred and fifty grams. After two months of incubation, a dark brown chick emerges. The offspring is regularly fed by its parents who, over a series of months, eventually end up feeding it two kilograms of food at a sitting, a quantity that requires foraging over hundreds of miles for days at a time. Such a large meal is almost grotesque. It fills the chick to bursting such that all it can do is sit and digest, looking

like nothing so much as an oily sack of feathers. The food, called chick oil, is formed of partly digested squid and crustaceans, a highly nutritious substance manufactured by the adults in the proventriculus of the stomach. This food gathering and delivery system allows the parents to collect and preserve large quantities of prey without having to return to the nest each time an item is caught. The maiden flight of the newly fledged chick occurs around December. The young bird must walk to the cliff edge at the end of the 'runway' and leap off in an impressive show of confidence. If luck is with it, it will disappear into the distance only to return four or five years later, ready to think about finding a mate.

On leaving the albatross, the trail winds along the cliff edge to overlook the famous blow-hole, a fissure in the lava which, when it receives the full force of the large Pacific swell, deflects an explosive burst of spray and water which funnels impressively, high into the air. Accompanied by a thunderous roar, the larger the swell which crashes against the island the greater the height of spray which gushes from the hole. Like staring into a

Kicker rock and roosting birds, San Cristóbal Island.

fire, there is something hypnotic about watching powerful waves beating relentlessly against a rocky shore, all the while seated at the edge of a cliff. Tourists pose to have their photographs taken while the marine iguanas and boobies look on unimpressed, having seen it all before.

Another dramatic natural feature of the southern isles is a gigantic rocky outcrop lying off the north shore of San Cristóbal Island. Kicker rock, or 'León Dormido' (Sleeping lion), as it is called in Spanish, is often the last of the visits made by passengers on a cruise from the Puerto Baquerizo Moreno airport. It is a fascinating structure, an old eroded tuff cone which glows orange in the morning light. The fascination lies in its shape, different from every angle, and its surface, home to hundreds of seabirds. With deep water all around, vessels are able to approach extremely close, with smaller yachts able to pass between the huge monoliths. The oldest of the present day Galapagos Islands, these southern isles, like those before them, will one day move further southeast and they, too, will submerge into oblivion, making room in the west for newer islands in their wake.

Masked booby, Española Island.

Kicker Rock, San Cristóbal Island.

Sunset, Punta Cormorant Lagoon, Floreana Island.

Pinnacle rock, Bartolomé Island.

Central Isles

The central isles of this chapter represent both the hub of tourist activity and the administrative and conservation nerve center in Galapagos. The principal islands we have concentrated on are Santiago, Sante Fe, Santa Cruz, South Plaza and lastly Bartolomé which, along with the Charles Darwin Research Station, is one of the most visited sites in the archipelago. The area around pinnacle rock, one of the classic Galapagos landmarks, also happens to be the best area of all in which to see the diminutive penguins so accustomed to our presence that they virtually ignore anybody in the water with them. It is a rare experience indeed to swim with penguins, and one reserved only for the brave in a penguin's more normal latitudes. That's not to say the water does not get cold. A thin wetsuit is actually a real pleasure in the islands and allows you to be much more comfortable for longer periods when snorkeling. Bartolomé is also a great area for white-tipped reef sharks and green turtles which use the beaches for nesting. Most of the other central isles also have very good snorkeling areas, including the beautiful bay at Santa Fe, Puerto Egas of

Santiago and North Plaza Island. Although Baltra, which is administered by the armed forces, has no official visitor site, it is probably visited by as many people as any other island. Tourists, having arrived at the island, are always eager to meet their boat and leave to begin their cruise, not really appreciating that they have made it to the archipelago. Baltra airport was first built as a US Air Force base in 1942 and maintained as a strategic point during World War II. Today it remains the principal airport serving the Galapagos, though only a few military personnel live on the island.

Anyone who has traveled to Santa Cruz via Baltra will remember that it is not an entirely straightforward process. After jostling for position in the scrum to receive luggage (unless you are travelling with a professionally escorted group), you must board a bus which will take you, for a small charge, to the Itabaca Channel. The last section of the road is somewhat worrying as the bus negotiates hairpin bends on a very steep incline. With luck, the ferry is waiting and, for another small fee and but a few minutes travel, you set foot onto the northern

One of the 'Gemelos' craters, Santa Cruz Island.

Spider, Santiago Island.

shores of Santa Cruz. There is no human habitation on the north of the island, and the town of Puerto Ayora, which is the main metropolis of the entire archipelago, lies on the far side to the south. This necessitates a bus journey which varies both according to the condition of the road and the bravado of the driver. In previous years, during a heavy El Niño season, the road has all but completely washed away, making access very difficult. Latterly however the well paved road now seems permanent. No matter how anxious the chauffeur is to return to town, one should count on at least an hour's drive. Some of the journey may at least be spent reading the stickers above the windscreen. Translated, they include such sayings as "God guides my way", "Daddy don't drive fast, we are waiting for you at home" and "Be cultured, throw your garbage out of the window".

The remainder of the journey is more profitably spent noticing the change in the vegetation zones which one must pass when traversing the island to the south. At sea level down near the channel, the vegetation is dominated by mangroves and saltbush, an area of mostly evergreen plants that pro-

Vermillion flycatcher and Spanish moss, Santa Cruz Island.

vide a false sense of lushness. Not determined so much by climatic factors, the strip of coastal plants are essentially those with a high salt tolerance. These areas are often of less interest to the botanist than other vegetation zones of the islands as the plants themselves show low levels of endemism.

As soon as the bus pulls away from the coast on its climb towards the center of the island, the greens of the mangroves dramatically disappear and the first of the climatically controlled vegetation zones becomes apparent - the arid zone. This is the most abundant vegetation type in the Galapagos and, along with the coastal strip, is the area in which most of the visitor-site trails are set. It is a semi-desert area covered in deciduous forest dominated by the *Bursera* sp. or *palo santo* (holy stick) trees. They, like all the plants of the arid zone, are drought resistant, with small leaves and deep roots. The *palo santos* spend much of the year with no leaves in a ghostly, deathlike, appearance. Their regular spacing, when seen from a distance, highlights the competition between individual trees for the scant water available. Interspersed among the *palo santos* are the characteristic dry zone plants; cacti such as *Opuntia* sp., or

Male yellow warbler, Bartolomé Island.

prickly pear, sprawl over the rocky soil while the elegant candelabra cactus, *Jasminocereus* sp., towers gracefully above the substrate. More prickly plants thrive in the area, including the gorse-like *Scutia pauciflora*, a dense, spiny green bush, along with one of the most attractive trees of the Galapagos, the *palo verde* (green stick). Although protected by heavy spines, the long sweeping green boughs, covered in compound leaves and tiny leaflets, distract the mind from the heavy armor. Growing with majestically arching branches reminiscent of a willow, even the trunk of this tree is green and capable of photosynthesis. The flowers are also attractive, being a rather showy yellow and orange in color.

With a slight increase in altitude as the bus continues on its journey, the plants begin to change. Like most things in nature, the transition is gradual. The aforementioned species slowly disappear to be replaced by a more heterogeneous mix of robust trees and thick tangled shrubs also deciduous in character. The increase in elevation brings with it greater levels of precipitation and even epiphytic plants, such as lichens, begin to appear. The

Saddle-back tortoise from Española Island, Charles Darwin Research Station, Santa Cruz Island.

Galapagos are essentially desert islands with two main seasons, a warm, wet season from January to June, and a cool, dry (or *garúa*) season from July to December. The prevailing trade winds in the Galapagos are from the southeast and, as they sweep over the ocean towards the islands, they pick up water. When the moisture-laden air meets an island of certain relief, it is forced upwards and over the island. As the air rises, it cools and, in cooling, its capacity to hold water diminishes, causing precipitation which either condenses to a fine mist called *garúa* or falls as rain. The southern sides of the islands are therefore the first to receive this bounty of fresh water and support lush vegetation growth. By the time the trade winds have pushed over the island to the northern side, most of the water is spent and the region is more arid due to this 'rain shadow' effect. As such, the arid and transition zones on the northern side of Santa Cruz are extended in area and altitude when compared with the equivalent regions in the south. Not only that, but fewer climatic and vegetation zones are present due to the more restricted water supply. Nevertheless, the transition zone,

Galapagos tortoise head, Charles Darwin Research Station, Santa Cruz Island.

containing such trees as the endemic *pega pega* (*Pisonia floribunda*) and *guayabillo* (*Psidium gala-pageium*), gives way, on the northern slopes of the island, to the *Scalesia* zone. This lush area of tall, spindly evergreen trees, related to sunflowers, is only present on the higher Galapagos Islands. *Scalesia* forms a forest, rather homogeneous in character, of a closed canopy up to fifteen meters in height. The understory is fairly open and contains many epiphytes as well as birds such as finches and flycatchers which also relish the habitat. Sadly, it is a seriously threatened ecosystem. Being such a fertile environment, it has been extensively cut by man and replaced with pasture on which to range livestock such as cattle and horses.

Driving out through the other side of the *Scalesia* zone, the vegetation opens up to an area of low growing ferns, sedges and grasses. This pampa zone at the top of the island receives more than two meters of precipitation in some years. At the summit of Santa Cruz the view looks out over a scene of lushness as the island dips south towards the coast. The pampa suddenly gives way to dense stands of an attractive, endemic shrub, *Miconia robinsoniana*,

Santa Fe land iguana, Santa Fe Island.

136

which in turn is surpassed by an area of vegetation dominated by *Zanthoxylum fagara*, or cat's claw, heavily draped with thick brown beards of epiphytic mosses and liverworts. As the bus continues careering down the hill, once again it passes through a thick stand of *Scalesia pedunculata*, the daisy tree, which tries to conceal two fabulous pit craters, one on either side of the road. The *Gemelos*, or twins as the craters are called, are huge in area and many tens of meters deep. The best theory as to their formation is that they were created by a series of collapses along circumferential fissures when magma from a large subterranean chamber was diverted to another area of the volcano via the immense system of underground lava tunnels throughout the island. As the now empty chambers could no longer support the heavy roof of rock, they proceeded to collapse. Surrounded by verdant growth, the *Gemelos* are a very pretty area, worth a visit by those with time on their hands while in Santa Cruz. A walk to the lookout point at the far end of the larger pit-crater is very rewarding. *Lycopodiums* line the cliff edge like minute Christmas trees while more endemic plants, *Scalesia* and *Darwiniothamnus*,

Galapagos land iguana, South Plaza Island.

Galapagos penguin hunting, Bartolomé Island.

Galapagos penguin, Bartolomé Island.

Sally lightfoot crabs mating, Santiago Island.

Oystercatcher eating Sally lightfoot crab, Santiago Island.

line the path. The keen observer may also be lucky enough to spot a short-eared owl which is often present in the area. Continuing down the hill, the ocean comes in and out of view as the bus negotiates fearsome corners. Fenceposts appear, occasionally decorated by a distinctive male vermillion flycatcher perched on their tops. The endemic plants give way to farmland and huge trees brought in from the mainland. They now line the road. Small towns appear and civilization instantly is upon you.

The sprawling town of Puerto Ayora begins a long way up the road, lining either side of its main artery. Before you know what has happened, the bus brakes to a dusty halt and people and bags begin spewing out onto the pavement. The heat of the town is somewhat oppressive after the misty cool of the highlands. There is a vibrant hustle-bustle of activity as people come to meet and greet the day's new arrivals. The town of Puerto Ayora is the largest of the Galapagos, with possibly as many as 16,000 residents. The commercial center comprises one main street and is lined almost its entire length with places to eat and T-shirt shops. In only the last decade, the growth of the town has been incredible.

White-tipped reef sharks in shallows, Bartolomé Island.

Since I went to guide in the islands in 1987 I have been saying that the Galapagos of tomorrow will resemble the Hawaii of today. Ten years ago there were just a few cars, trucks and buses which slowly negotiated the dusty dirt road. Gasoline was stored at people's homes in fifty-five gallon drums and replenished each time the ship came to port. The atmosphere was casual and people seemed happy. They had only come in the first place because they wanted to be there. Today, as progress has swept through the community like a tidal wave, attitudes have changed, the roads are paved to accommodate the large volume of traffic, including 700 taxies, fueled by modern gasoline facilities, which race around the one way circuit hurrying to do business. Monetary transactions are now facilitated by satellite banking communications. Instead of the once laid back lifestyle the air is now filled with a palpable electricity. The exponential population growth is putting pressure on natural and human resources alike, discontent and social unrest is rife as the lower classes struggle to make a living. Recent instability in local government institutions has done little to help the situation. Tourism is by far the mainstay of the economy within the islands, except for the huge clandestine wealth being generated by a few in illegal fishing and other illicit industries. The harbor hums to the sound of outboard engines ferrying tourists from their live-aboard yachts to shore. One of the most important things on their minds while in Santa Cruz seems to be to stock up on a collection of souvenir T-shirts with which to impress friends back home. The second, and more important, reason for visiting the town is to visit the Charles Darwin Research Station. Here, in a recently upgraded facility, visitors are led by their guide through an excellent series of educational displays. The main thrust of the section open to the public is to highlight the extremely successful and long standing tortoise repatriation program. Since its early beginnings, more than 3,000 young tortoises have been reintro-

Sea cucumber, Bartolomé Island.

Galapagos fur seal, Santiago Island.

Galapagos fur seal, Santiago Island.

Inset: Green turtle laying eggs, Baltra Island.
Green turtle digging nest pit, Baltra Island.

duced to their original habitats – an impressive effort. After having been reared in the station's facilities, they are rat or dog proof (dependent on the particular threat on their native island), and are deemed ready for reintroduction. It has been to date a fabulous success. One story especially worthy of mention is the case of the Española population which was reduced at one point to only fourteen individuals (2 males and 12 females) so thinly spread out on the island that they probably seldom, if ever, met to breed. It was decided to bring them all into the station for breeding purposes. Eventually, with the aid of a third, particularly vigorous, stud male repatriated from San Diego Zoo, more than 1,300 individuals have been released back onto Española, leaving us with the hope that one day we will be watching courting albatross and suddenly be surprised by a healthy giant tortoise lumbering through as it always should have been.

Turtle returning to sea after egg laying.

As mentioned in the introduction, introduced flora and fauna pose some of the most serious threats to the health of the park. Both the Charles Darwin Research Station (CDRS) and the Galapagos National Park Service (GNPS) are tremendously committed to reversing the legacy of human intervention. Both institutions have traditionally been so strapped for cash that nothing was easy. (The economics have improved lately, with the national park now retaining a higher percentage of the entrance fee.) Nevertheless, a momentous breakthrough in 2004 was the complete eradication of pigs and donkeys on Santiago Island. In a near super-human effort, the national park guards, with their teams of male-only dogs (to prevent accidental introductions of viable populations), have overcome the rough lava terrain, the hordes of introduced fire ants, tangled, spiny vegetation and extreme heat and lack of water to reduce the total island pig population to zero. The next challenge will be the final phase of the removal of the goat population, another daunting prospect. With their extremely rapid

Sea lion in long green grass, El Niño 1998, South Plaza Island.

Lava lizard eating scorpion, Santiago Island.

Bull Galapagos fur seal, Santiago Island.

reproduction rates, goats are a nightmare to extirpate totally. An introduction of only three goats on Pinta in the late 1950s, for example, led to a population of over 400,000 by 1970! However with cutting-edge technology, including the use of Judas goats, GIS tracking and helicopters the efforts are well on the way to becoming completely successful. (Currently there is an extensive campaign, Project Isabela, to not only rid Alcedo volcano of its huge, recent goat population but also to restore the entire island to a more natural state. Again, a combined GNPS and CDRS project.) There are innumerable other projects on the go, such as land iguana breeding and repatriation programs, exotic plant eradication programs and also a heavy emphasis on local environmental education programs. Both institutions are doing a fabulous job, particularly considering their means. The CDRS relies heavily on foreign donations and it is here that you are able to help. A list of organizations receiving donations towards Galapagos conservation projects appears in Appendix B.

Giant Opuntia cactus, Santa Fe Island.

Glossary

Careen
To haul a vessel onto a beach or dry area where it is turned on its side for maintenance and repair.

Cloaca
Opening in birds, reptiles and amphibians of genital and excretory organs.

Coriolis force
The force exerted on fluids (in this case) due to the rotation of the earth.

Endemic
An animal or plant is endemic to a specified area if it occurs naturally in that area and nowhere else.

Garúa
Local name for a fine mist forming in elevated portions of the Galapagos usually between July and December.

Morph
A variant.

Niche
The specific role of an organism within its environment.

Osmosis
The transfer of a concentrated solution to a less concentrated solution through a semi-permeable membrane.

Panga
Local Galapagos term for a small dingy.

Parasitic cone
A volcanic cone forming on the flank of a larger volcano.

Pelagic
Organisms of open ocean.

Photosynthesis
The process whereby plants use sunlight to convert carbon dioxide into organic compounds in order to grow.

Pinniped
Mammals of the seal family which includes walruses, seals, sea lions and fur seals.

Tectonic Plate
A rigid section of the earth's crust or ocean floor which drifts in relation to other tectonic plates in response to convection currents within the mantle of the earth.

Thigmotactic
Seeking body contact.

Female magnificent frigatebird, Fernandina Island.

Bibliography

Anhalzer, J.J. National Parks of Ecuador. Quito, Ecuador: Imprenta Mariscal.

Beebe, W. 1924. Galapagos - World's End. London, New York: C.P. Putman.

Boyce, B. 1994. A Traveller's Guide to the Galapagos Islands. Galapagos Travel, San Jose, CA.

Castro, I and A. Phillips. 1996. A Guide to The Birds of the Galapagos Islands. Princeton University Press.

Constant, P. 1992. Marine Life of the Galapagos. A Guide to the Fishes, Whales, Dolphins and other Marine Mammals. Production House.

Corral, C., Corral, P., Oxford, P. 1998. Ecuador Spaces of Light. Quito, Ecuador: Imprenta Mariscal.

Cribb, J. 1986. Subtidal Galapagos, Exploring the Waters of Darwin's Islands. Camden House Publishing Ltd.

Darwin, C. 1845. The Voyage of the Beagle. Journal of researches into the Natural History and Geology of the Countries visited during the Voyage round the World of H.M.S. 'Beagle' under command of Captain FitzRoy, R.N. John Murray. London.

Darwin, C. 1859. On the Origin of Species. John Murray. London.

De Roy, T. and M. Jones, 1990. Portraits of Galapagos. Quito, Ecuador: Imprenta Mariscal

De Roy, T. 1998. Galapagos: Islands Born of Fire. Quito, Ecuador: Libri Mundi.

Grant, P.R. 1986. Ecology and Evolution of Darwin's Finches. New Jersey: Princeton University Press.

Grant, B.R. and P.R. Grant. 1989. Evolutionary Dynamics of a Natural Population. The Large Cactus Finch of the Galapagos. The University of Chicago Press.

Grove, J.S., S. García and S. Massey. 1984. Lista de los peces de Galápagos. Guayaquil, Ecuador: Boletín Científico Y Técnico, Instituto Nacional de Pesca.

Grove, J.S., R.J. Lavenberg, 1997. The Fishes of the Galapagos Islands. Standford University Press.

Harris, M.P. 1974. A Field Guide to the Birds of the Galapagos. London: Collins.

Harrison, P. 1983. Seabirds an Identification Guide. Christopher Helm. London.

Hickman, J. 1985. The Enchanted Islands. The Galapagos Discovered. Anthony Nelson Ltd.

Hickin, N.E., Animal Life of the Galapagos.

Horwell, D., P. Oxford. 1999. Galapagos Wildlife. Bucks, England: Bradt Publications.

Humann, P. 1993. Reef Fish Identification. Galapagos. Quito, Ecuador: Libri Mundi.

Jackson, M. H. 1993. Galapagos, a Natural History. Calgary: The University of Calgary Press.

Lack, D.1947 Darwin's Finches. London: Cambridge University Press.

Leatherwood, S., R.R. Reeves. 1983. The Sierra Club Handbook of Whales and Dolphins. San Francisco: Sierra Club Books.

Merlin, G. 1988. A Field Guide to the Fishes of Galapagos. Quito, Ecuador: Imprenta Mariscal

Moore, A., and T. Moore. 1980. Guide to the Visitor Sites of Parque Nacional Galápagos. Servicio Parque Nacional. Galápagos, Ecuador.

Moore, T. 1980. Galapagos Islands Lost in Time. New York: Viking Press.

Moorhead, A. 1971. Darwin and the Beagle. Harmondsworth, Penguin, England.

Nelson, J.B. 1978. The Sulidae. London: Oxford University Press.

Nelson, B. 1968. Galapagos. Islands of Birds. Longmans Green and Co. Ltd.

Patzelt, E. 1989. Fauna del Ecuador. Quito, Ecuador: Ediciones del Banco Central.

Perry, R. 1984. Galapagos. - (Key Environments) Oxford: Pergamon Press Ltd.

Quammen, D. 1997. The Song of the Dodo. New York: Touchstone.

Reeves, R.R., B.S. Stewart, S. Leatherwood. 1992. The Sierra Club Handbook of Seals and Sirenians. San Francisco: Sierra Club Books.

Ryan, P.R. 1987. Oceanus, the International Magazine of Marine Science and Policy. Vol 30. Number 2. Woods Hole Oceanographic Institute.

Schofield, E.K. 1970. Field Guide to Some Common Galapagos Plants. Columbus: Ohio State University Research Foundation.

Schönitzer, K. Galapagos Plants. Contribution Number 172 of the Charles Darwin Foundation.

Shaw, J. 1984. The Nature Photographers' Complete Guide to Professional Field Techniques. New York: Amphoto, American Photographic Book Publishing. Ltd.

Steadman, D.W. and S. Zousmer. 1988. Galapagos Discovery on Darwin's Islands. Smithsonian Institution Press.

Thornton, I. 1971. Darwin's Islands; A Natural History of the Galapagos Islands. Garden City, New York: Natural History Press.

Treherne, J.E. 1983. The Galapagos Affair. London: Jonathan Cape.

The Charles Darwin Foundation for the Galapagos Islands. Annual Report, 2004.

Wellington, G.M. 1975. The Galapagos Coastal Marine Environments. Ph.D. Thesis. Galapagos: Charles Darwin Research Station.

Weiner, J. 1995. The Beak of the Finch. A Story of Evolution in Our Time. England: Vintage.

Wiggins, I.L., and D.M. Porter. 1971. Flora of the Galapagos Islands. Stanford University Press.

Wittmer, M. 1989. Floreana. Quito, Ecuador: Libri Mundi.

Yépez, V., P. Díaz, L. S. Rodríguez, (INEFAN-GEF). 1998. Guía de Parques Nacionales y Reservas del Ecuador. Quito, Ecuador: INEFAN.

Appendix A

Rules and Guidelines of the National Park

1. Do not remove or disturb any plant, rock or animal on the islands.
2. Be careful not to transport any live material to the islands or from island to island. Check your clothing for seeds and insects before disembarking the ship for shore.
3. Do not touch the animals.
4. Do not feed the animals.
5. Always remain on the path where designated.
6. Always remain with your guide where required.
7. Do not startle or chase any animal from its nest or resting place. Be extremely careful in and around breeding colonies.
8. Do not force your way through dense bush or thickets. This will destroy the plant life and seeds may become lodged on your person.
9. Do not litter on land or from the vessel whilst at sea.
10. Do not buy souvenirs made from any native animal part, coral or plant except certain wood.
11. Do not write graffiti or deface rocks and plants on the islands.
12. Do not hesitate to show your conservationist attitude and explain to others the rules. Notify the National Park Service if you see any damage being done.

Galapagos hawk, Española Island.

Appendix B

Institutions

Charles Darwin Foundation, Inc.
407 North Washington Street, Suite 105
Falls Church, VA 22046, USA.
tel: +1 703 538 6833
e-mail: *darwin@galapagos.org*
www.galapagos.org

Zoologische Gesellschaft Frankfurt
Alfred-Brehm-Platz 16
D-60316 Frankfurt, Germany.
Spenden mit dem Hinweis "Galapagos" an: Frankfurter
Sparkasse BLZ 500 502 01, Kontonummer: 80002.
e-mail: *info@zgf.de*
www.zgf.de

Stichting Vrienden van de Galapagos Eilanden
c/o Mevr. E. Boele-de Jong
Mendelssohnstraat 13
3281 VH Numansdorp, The Netherlands.
tel: +31 186 651590
e-mail: *secr.galapagos@hetnet.nl*
www.galapagos.nl

The Charles Darwin Research Station
Puerto Ayora, Isla Santa Cruz,
Galapagos, Ecuador.
tel: +593 5 2526651
e-mail: *infocdrs@fcdarwin.org*

Nordic Friends of Galapagos
Korkeasaari
00570 Helsinki, Finland.
tel: +358 50 5644279
e-mail: *k.kumenius@kolumbus.fi*
www.galapagosnordic.fi

Galapagos Conservation Trust
5 Derby Street
London W1Y 7AD, UK.
tel: +44 (0) 20 7629 5049
e-mail: *gct@gct.org*
www.gct.org

The Galapagos Darwin Trust
Banque Internationale à Luxembourg
2, Boulevard Royal
L-2953 Luxembourg.
Donations marked "For the Galapagos" may be made
to Account No. 1-100/9071.

Freunde der Galapagos Inseln (CH)
c/o Zoo Zürich
Zürichbergstr. 221
CH-8044 Zürich, Switzerland.
tel: +41 (0) 1 254 26 70
e-mail: *galapagos@zoo.ch*
www.galapagos-ch.org

Acknowledgements

When first arriving to take a job on the coast of mainland Ecuador in 1985, it was with a sense of longing that I looked west across the ocean towards the distant and magical Galapagos Islands beyond the horizon. In 1987 I moved to the Galapagos to become a naturalist guide. It is during that time that I made many valued friends. I would like to express my deepest gratitude to the following people, Carmen Angermeyer, Fiddi Angermeyer, Eliécer Cruz, Felipe Cruz, Georgina Cruz, the late Gayle Davis Merlen, David Day, Jacqueline De Roy, Tui De Roy, Andy Drumm, Sylvia Harcourt, Mark Jones, Godfrey Merlen, Jack Nelson, the Schiess family, Graham Watkins, the Galapagos National Park Service and the Charles Darwin Research Station.

As a couple, Reneé and I would like to thank our loyal friends on mainland Ecuador. They include Dorothy Albright, Beny Ammeter, Juan Lorenzo Barragán, María Elena Barragán, Colleen Berlin, Jean Brown, Ximena Benavides, Andrés & Andrea Bustamante, Ben Dodd, Patricio and Ivette Jiménez, László Károlyi, Julian Larrea, Belen Mena, Lisanne Newport, Gary Parkin, Tom Quesenberry, Ana Lucía Sosa, Clarice Strang, Lucho Suarez, Andrea Tamayo, Mariela Tenorio, Kristina Tronstad, Sally Vergette, Charlie and Sherry Vogt, Andy Watkins, Ellen and Phil Whitaker and Guillermo and Roxana Zaldumbide.

Our special thanks also go to Marcela Garcia of Libri Mundi, Paco Valdivieso of Imprenta Mariscal and also to his team, particularly Andy Valdivieso, Gustavo Moya, and Jaime Mosquera; Juan Lorenzo Barragán and Lorena Zurita of Azuca, for an excellent design; Mary Ellen Fieweger, for her red pen and grammatical mangle through which she squeezed the text and to Graham Watkins for his vision and dedication to the islands.

As always our love goes out to our families who continue to encourage our endeavors from their farflung corners of the planet.

Pete Oxford and Reneé Bish,
Quito, Ecuador 2005

Sleeping sea lion, Española Island.